NINE HALLMARKS OF HIGHLY INCOMPETENT LOSERS™

Pat Reeder

with Laura Ainsworth

Foreword by Mike Huckabee

Illustrations by Laura Ainsworth

www.comedy-wire.com

Published by Comedy Wire Inc.

For information on booking the authors for speaking engagements, visit www.comedy-wire.com, e-mail pat@comedy-wire.com, or write to Comedy Wire Inc at the address above.

First Edition: © May 2002
Revised E-book Editions: © Nov. 2013, Nov. 2015

ISBN-10: 0615939678

ISBN-13: 978-0615939674 (Comedy Wire Inc.)

Dedication

To Laura,
for her love and inspiration,
her great drawings,
and half the good lines...

And to all the people of the world who work
so hard doing dumb things every day,
just to keep us in business...

TABLE OF CONTENTS

FOREWORD

Pat Reeder and Laura Ainsworth's *Comedy Wire* is as much a part of my morning reading routine as the Bible and the morning paper. It may not be as important as the Bible, but it sure as heck is more pleasurable than the morning paper.

Pat and Laura stay up all night while the rest of us sleep, and they "find the funny" in the serious news as well as dig out things that reveal that some people are simply so stupid that the punch line doesn't even need to be pointed out.

If you are one of those hideous politically-correct people who believe that the rest of us live "down sewer" from you, then you're going to hate this book. It's not for pretentious snobs who fear that a deep guffaw will be "undignified." It's for those of us who get through life by laughing out loud and not really caring who "gets it" and who doesn't.

In my world of the full contact sport of politics and public office, a sense of humor is as necessary as a roomful of lobbyists lined up to hand over big checks for the campaign. This book is a million dollars worth of laughs, and it doesn't cost that much, and you get to skip the finger food.

In the interest of full disclosure, I confess that some mornings, I've hated Pat and Laura as well — those days when I laughed so hard, I spewed coffee all over my computer keyboard or had to change shirts or (please don't tell this!) pants.

Read this book on days when you really feel down on yourself. You'll be lifted up knowing that there are other people who really are dumber than you feel!

Laughing Out Loud,

Mike Huckabee

Former Arkansas Governor and host of Fox News' *Huckabee* & Cumulus Media's *The Huckabee Report*

INTRODUCTION

When I sat down to write this book, I intended to embark on a serious examination of a subject that is of vital importance to every business person in our fast-paced, modern world. That subject was competence.

Unfortunately, I hit the wrong combination of button thingies on my keyboard, and the "competence" manuscript went *"Pff-ffffffft!"*

However, as I was discussing my dilemma with the very nice fireman who came to extinguish my hard drive, we both agreed that there is a far stronger and more prevalent force than competence influencing daily events — a force that should be of even greater concern to every business person in our fast-paced, modern world.

That force is *incompetence.*

You see, the two of us — he as a firefighter, I as a topical comedy writer — concluded that without good old-fashioned human idiocy, we would both be out of a job.

Fortunately, I had already spent most of my life pursuing a personal, in-depth study of human incompetence.

From the time I was a small boy and began collecting "Blooper" records and books, I have always been fascinated with mistakes. I find it enthralling to ponder the seemingly limitless variety of ways in which people screw things up. I have an insatiable curiosity about the mistakes people make, why they make them, how they overcome them, and most importantly, whether we can avoid making our own mistakes by studying and learning from other people's.

So besotted was I with this subject that during high school, while my classmates were driving to dances, pep rallies and football games, I once drove 40 miles to hear a lecture by Dr. Laurence J. Peter, creator of *The Peter Principle* ("In a hierarchy, people tend to rise to their level of incompetence and stay there"). And if you think I did this just because it made me popular with the other kids, then you are sadly mistaken.

After college, I spent over a decade working in corporate communications, where my appetite for spotting incompetence and stupidity enjoyed gluttonous daily feedings. I spent over a decade working for such major companies as GTE, Sylvania and DLM Inc., writing everything from sales role-play videos (i.e., illustrating what sales people were doing wrong to help them learn how to do it right) to speeches for executives, which usually meant translating nearly-impenetrable MBA corpo-jargonspeak into plain English.

I soon found myself specializing in making complicated things understandable to people who didn't have a clue. For instance, I wrote a number of humorous instructional videos for laymen on every topic from using the latest computer software programs to buying a house, all of which required me to tackle a complicated subject with no prior knowledge, monkey around and make all the mistakes that other neophytes might bumble into, then explain clearly and simply how to avoid them. I was even the head writer for the original home video episodes of *Barney the Dinosaur,* for which my well-honed ability to communicate on a four-year-old level really came in handy.

As a sideline, I have written, voiced and produced hundreds of radio commercials for every type of business.

One client is a jewelry store owner in Connecticut who provided me with an early epiphany. I first called on her with a saleswoman from a local radio station, who warned me that she was so demanding, she would be impossible to get along with. Naturally, we ended up talking for hours, became best friends, and I still do all her radio advertising. Much later, she confided to me that ad agencies had been trying to sell her for years, but she always turned them down because they never listened to her business philosophy or gave her anything that reflected it. She said, "You were the first person who ever walked through the door who had a brain."

While modesty prevents me from believing that (doctors assure me that anyone would need a brain just to turn the doorknob), it did confirm my theory about how widespread incompetence is.

This was further confirmed by the experiences of other acquaintances of mine, such as the exhausted radio producer who quit his dream job in Los Angeles overseeing a national talk show and moved back to Texas because everyone else in his company came in at 11, took a two-hour lunch, then left at 4. Or the hotel construction manager in Las Vegas who offered to teach me his business from scratch if I would just come work for him, because (deja vu), "I can't find anybody with a brain!" I heard this lament so many times that I began to suspect the world didn't need another self-help guru, it needed the Wizard of Oz.

Eventually, I shifted from corporate communications into full-time, intentional comedy writing for the entertainment industry, but my longtime fascination with incompetence and failure continued to entwine itself with my work. For instance, I spent several years interviewing non-singing celebrities about why they thought it was a good career move to record their croaking for posterity for my previous book, *Hollywood Hi-Fi.*

Finally, for a number of years, my wife Laura Ainsworth and I wrote our own syndicated radio prep service, *The Comedy Wire* (www.comedy-wire.com) and now do similar writing on contract for nationally-syndicated radio and Internet shows. We spent the better part of each day scouring newspapers, magazines, TV and the Internet and weeding through e-mails from our worldwide network of radio DJs, talk show hosts, standup comics, webmasters, PR agents and political insiders, searching for unusual news stories that would be good grist for humorous commentary. Naturally, the ones that most intrigued me involved somebody doing something supremely stupid.

Over the years, we have squirreled away thousands of these stories. After so much time and study, I think it's safe to say that I have become one of the world's leading experts on the lack of expertise. And if there is anything I don't know about ignorance, well...I don't know what it would be.

In dealing with so many of these tales of boobery, we began spotting similarities between even the most disparate stories of failure and humiliation. The details may be unique and the events occur in widely-scattered locations and involve people of many diverse cultures and economic stations, but we realized that the vast majority of these stories, when boiled down to their essence, are merely variations on one or more of nine basic, common mistakes that people make over and over again.

And so, we began separating these stories into our own broad categories of boneheaded missteps, or as we like to call them, *Nine Hallmarks of Highly Incompetent Losers.*

It is often said that mistakes are good, because that is how we learn. People who say that are mistaken.

Mistakes may be how we learn, but they are also how we get fired, go bankrupt, and end up in prison. Incarceration can really take the fun out of learning. Besides, if your boss truly considered mistakes to be learning experiences, then the biggest screw-up in the company would get promoted repeatedly, and that only happens to the boss's son-in-law.

One thing that sets people apart from animals is that we (or some of us, at least) have the ability to learn from the mistakes of others. It isn't necessary for us to make every possible mistake personally to learn something from it. This process starts at an early age. Most of us had mothers who warned us, "Don't touch the stove, it's hot!" And how many of us touched it anyway? (Just hold up as many fingers as you've still got.) Who knows, maybe we wouldn't have touched that hot stove if, as toddlers, we had been able to watch our big brother touch it first, then giggle adorably as he ran screaming from the room.

Well, that's what I intend to do with this book. No, not make you run screaming from the room. I intend to share some of the most entertainingly idiotic goofs, foul-ups and boo-boos from our vast files and point out the common, recurring mistakes that underlie them. While the examples may be humorous, the advice is sound. I hope that I can help you achieve a happier personal life and a more successful career simply by learning to avoid the obvious, preventable human errors that led to the embarrassment and failure these poor chuckleheads endured. In short, I am going to teach you how to do things wrong, in hopes that, like most people who read self-help books, you will immediately go forth and do the opposite of what you were told.

Incidentally, while I jovially call these recurring mistakes *Nine Hallmarks of Highly Incompetent Losers,* please understand I do not mean to imply that the people in these news stories I quote are genuinely hopeless losers.

They should perish that thought, and so should their libel attorneys. Most likely, these are just ordinary folks who had an off-day, or week, or year. They made a simple, all-too-human mistake — albeit one that required the dialing of 911 — and some meddling busybody alerted the media. What can one do but laugh? And, of course, learn from it.

Anyone can make at least one boneheaded move. For instance, I made a conscious decision to become a writer. For a *living!* Let that be your first tip about what to avoid if you want to be rich and successful.

And now, let's turn our attention to all the other poor losers out there, so we can learn how not to join them.

HALLMARK #1: NEVER PLAN AHEAD

If there is any general rule that deserves to be ranked #1 for those who truly wish to become incompetent failures, it has to be this one: "Never plan ahead."

I'm not talking about the type of planning ahead you are normally urged to do in self-help books, such as planning your retirement portfolio while you're still struggling to master training pants. I mean the most basic, "which-foot-shall-I-put-out-in-front-of-me-next?" type of planning ahead.

Over the past decade, I can't tell you how many times I've received this same basic story from all over the world:

A would-be burglar has seen one too many *Die Hard* movies and assumes air conditioning ducts are big enough for Bruce Willis and a sidekick to crawl through side-by-side while exchanging snappy repartee. So the thief tries to break into a store by crawling through an a/c duct and gets stuck. My friend the fireman is called to come spray a little WD-40 on his spare tire and yank him out. I've heard this yarn so many times, I don't even bother to make fun of it anymore.

Okay, except for this one: some twit in Tampa, Florida, tried to break into a store through the vent and got stuck with his legs dangling from the ceiling. It was late at night, so he assumed the store would be closed. He also hadn't planned ahead enough to bother finding out that the store was a 7-11 that was open 24 hours a day. It was quite crowded when he performed his surprise imitation of a breach birth. Worse, his legs burst through the ceiling directly above the donut counter. Take a wild guess who would be standing at a 7-11 donut counter at 2 a.m. That's right: two cops.

Even I had to concede, this took poor planning to a whole new level.

Fortunately, I have never suffered any shortage of wonderfully diverse anecdotes that illustrate the dangers of failing to plan for all the conceivable consequences before taking action. Here are just a few...

• A man in Onesti, Romania, shampooed his hair with gasoline to kill his lice, then decided to dry his hair by leaning over his wood-burning stove. His wife saved his life by putting out his flaming head with blankets. I'm forced to admit this plan did kill the lice.

• A thief in Damianiovo, Bulgaria, worked for four hours cutting through barbed wire at a large cooperative farm, then disabling the alarm system and cracking the safe. But he had failed to find out beforehand what was inside. He escaped with the entire contents of the safe: the Bulgarian equivalent of $4.30. He actually would've made a higher hourly wage by working on a Bulgarian cooperative farm.

• In Columbus, Ohio, a would-be bank robber who failed to do his research entered a National City Bank branch and handed the teller a note demanding money. She told him they had no money at that branch because it existed solely to take loan applications. He insisted she open all the drawers. She did. There was no money in any of them. He fled but was later captured. I like to think by the Loan Arranger.

• In Seattle, a would-be burglar used a tall ladder to enter a locked warehouse through a high window and jump down to the floor. Only after he was inside did he realize that he couldn't get back up to the window to escape because his ladder was still leaning against the outside of the building. He had to call a fire crew to rescue him. While he waited, he stole a box of cigarettes and smoked them. No wonder he didn't have enough stamina to haul himself up to the window.

• A convicted burglar at Elmwood prison in Milpitas, California, planned a nearly-perfect escape. He pried some bars apart one night, wiggled through a skylight above his cell and ran across the yard. But he jumped over the wrong fence. Instead of landing outside and gaining his freedom, he landed next door — in the Elmwood Women's Prison. Of course, it's possible this wasn't a mistake.

• In Johnson County, Texas, a 22-year-old drifter tried to steal a fully-loaded Union Pacific freight train, but couldn't get the brake off. So he used the radio to call dispatchers and ask them if they could tell him how to release the brake. Instead, they called the sheriff, who arrested him for felony theft. He told police that he had wanted to go "wherever the train takes me," but he ended up going where the prison bus took him.

• A 21-year-old man who was wanted for a number of thefts was caught by police in Transcona, Canada, when his car ran out of gas in the middle of an intersection. The car was stolen, he had a knife and a mask on the seat, and he was on his way to rob a gas station. A police spokesman said it was "pretty dumb" to drive off to rob a gas station without first making sure you have enough gas to get there and to escape. It's also pretty dumb to steal a getaway car that's out of gas.

• A gang in New York City tried to rob an armored car, but one member overslept, another forgot his gun, and they had car trouble on the way to commit the crime. They were intercepted by FBI agents, who had to wake up one of them to read him his rights. In this case, poor planning had an upside: the judge told the gang leader that if the robbery had been successful, he would have spent 14 years in prison, but since he was so incompetent, the judge gave him just 41 months. Apparently, the judge feared that if he spent too much time in prison, he might actually learn how to be a criminal.

Okay, I know what you're thinking at this point: "Pat, those stories are all about men who were on their own or hanging out with their buds. As any woman who's ever left her husband alone for a weekend knows, a guy in that situation can always think up something stupid to do and get in trouble."

Ah, but you don't have to worry about that! You work for a big company or a large government agency. You're surrounded by dozens, even hundreds of intelligent people; college-educated professionals who work together on multi-million-dollar projects. You could never be sunk by something as dumb as poor planning.

To which I would respond with three letters: "XFL."

While you're looking up the Xtreme Football League on Wikipedia, I'll have a sip of New Coke, check the Enron stocks Bernie Madoff bought for me, gas up my Edsel and sign up for Obamacare.

The fact is, no organization, no matter how big or sophisticated, is immune to the pitfalls of bad planning. Here are a few examples of what can be accomplished when a large group of professionals pool their talents and resources to spend a mountain of money on a poorly-planned project...

• France spent 14 years and billions of francs to construct the only French aircraft carrier, the *Charles de Gaulle,* which upon its launch turned out to be truly French, in that it was apparently held together by spit. The flight deck was too short, the crew couldn't see through the armored glass, the washing machines made the whole ship vibrate, a propeller broke off during its maiden voyage, and a mysterious fire at the factory destroyed all records about the making of the propeller. France was forced to revert to Defense Plan B: "Call America."

• Less than a year after its much-ballyhooed opening, Great Britain's gigantic Millennium Dome had attracted so few visitors, it was earmarked for closure and its exhibits sold at auction to recoup some of the taxpayers' money. Among the leftovers which the government inexplicably thought would prove irresistible to tourists were some foot-long models of body lice, which sold for $145 each to an antique dealer who planned to use them to upset his wife and children. A six-foot model of a hamster sold for $4,500, while a giant brain fetched only $1,700. But it was obvious from this whole project that Britons don't attach much value to owning a very large brain.

• Officials at Germany's Dessau Prison decided to teach the inmates a trade to give them a head start on life outside prison. So they got the bright idea to start a welding class. Four prisoners signed up and worked together on a class project: they built a ladder and used it to escape prison. But the class could be deemed a success since it did give them a head start on life outside prison.

• One of Israel's leading architects was hired to create a new library for Israel's Academic Engineering College. He hoped to show off by filling it with his unique design ideas, including strips of clear Lucite in the floors and ceilings to let in sunlight all the way down from the roof to the lobby. Only after it was built did he realize that men on lower floors would be able to look right up the skirts of women on the floors above them. The brilliant architect admitted that he had gotten so wrapped up in "innovative computerized planning" that he never stopped to think about why women object to glass ceilings.

As these examples show, poor planning can sink any project, no matter how big. The only difference between those poor burglars stuck in the air shafts and big government agencies and corporations is that when governments and corporations screw up, everybody gets the shaft.

Let me give you one more example to hammer the point home: Go to your refrigerator and see if you have any nice, cold Napa Naturals. You don't? I'm surprised, because that was a very popular beverage — for about six months.

Back in 1983, some entrepreneurs in California's Napa Valley noticed that people were shelling out $3 for a little bottle of water because it came from France. They figured that if yuppies would pay that much for water, surely they'd pay at least as much for a healthy drink containing actual flavor molecules. So they formed a beverage company and did everything that a business manual writer could suggest. They raised over $8 million in start-up capital, they hired the marketing team that introduced Perrier to the US, they lined up production facilities and distribution routes, they got shelf space in stores, and most importantly, they developed a product that focus groups loved: Napa Naturals, the world's first natural soft drink — 67 percent real fruit juice, delicious and with no preservatives.

They hit the market in January of 1984 and were an immediate smash. Within six months, they'd broken Perrier's American sales record. So why aren't you quaffing a Napa Natural right now?

Because the company went bankrupt when, halfway through 1984, something totally unforeseen occurred.

Summer arrived.

Science Quiz: When you combine summer heat, a sealed can, fruit juice and no preservatives, what happens? That's right: a wondrous process called "fermentation" begins. And all across America, Napa Naturals began exploding off the shelves — this time, literally.

There was a recall and the recipe was changed to cut back on gaseous outbursts, but by then, the damage was done. Grocers were afraid to put it back on their shelves. They thought it was a time bomb — or more precisely, a wine bomb.

The product went from boom to *BOOM!* in six short months, all because the makers failed to plan for one little thing that any high school science student or hillbilly moonshiner could have warned them about.

Why didn't they spot it? I believe it's because everyone at the company thought that everyone else was such an expert in his field that nobody bothered thinking outside his or her own specialty. Each person concentrated on one area of expertise — sales, marketing, distribution, etc. — and never considered the big picture. Nobody planned far enough ahead to ponder what new conditions might arise in just six months.

In other words, none of those highly-trained professionals and Harvard MBAs ever considered that when summer arrives, it gets hot.

That guy with his legs sticking through the 7-11 ceiling doesn't seem like such a dunce now, does he?

TRANSLATION:
IF YOU HAVE THIS PERMIT,
YOU MUST PARK
IN A HANDICAPPED SPACE!

HALLMARK #2: LOSE SIGHT OF YOUR GOAL

Let's say you've absorbed Loser Hallmark #1 and have planned ahead carefully. You know what your goal is and how you plan to accomplish it in detail. Nothing can go wrong now, right?

Oh, you adorable, cockeyed optimist! That's like saying you made meticulous plans before going whitewater rafting, even tracing your route on a map with a red marker, so nothing could possibly go wrong. Well, that's exactly what Ned Beatty did in *Deliverance*.

Having set down your goal and your plan to achieve it, you now go jitterbugging into a minefield of dire possibilities. The one you will most likely encounter next is the Second Hallmark of the Incompetent Loser: "Losing Sight of the Goal."

Again, to illustrate this on the simplest level, let's first look at the world's simplest people: small time crooks...

- A thief broke into a house in Juneau, Alaska, with the simple and obvious goal of robbing it. But he became so excited when he found some fresh-baked cinnamon sticky buns in the house, he just had to pick up the homeowner's phone and call a friend to tell him about the great breakfast he'd stolen. He mistakenly punched a speed dial button that called 911 and brought the police. Who, of course, came running when he told them about the fresh-baked sticky buns.

- A burglar in the northern US robbed a house in the middle of winter and might have gotten away with it, except he could not resist stopping outside and writing his name in the snow on the lawn with urine. Upon his

arrest, he told police, "I am so stupid." But at least he
had good penmanship.

• A man was on trial in Seattle, pleading innocent to a
charge that he had attacked his estranged wife, when
he suddenly rushed the witness stand, hit her and tried
to strangle her. Bailiffs had to use pepper spray to get
him off her. The Associated Press reported that this
"may" have hurt his case. His lawyer asked that the
jury be dismissed because they had witnessed the
attack, which might inexplicably prejudice their
verdict. Besides, they would be too busy being
witnesses in his *next* trial for attacking his wife.

• In Sacramento, California, two men suspected of
robbing at least 16 banks were finally captured by the
FBI when one entered a bank to rob it, and the other
decided that would be the perfect moment to go run the
getaway car through a car wash. Their hopes for a
clean getaway were dashed when the washing took
longer than expected. They were captured while still
waiting for their car to emerge, thus teaching them a
valuable lesson: when you're in a hurry, don't opt for
the hot wax.

Of course, these situations arose primarily from sheer stupidity.
Among higher life forms, it is more likely that people will lose sight
of their goal because they are more focused on working toward the
goal than on achieving it. They become so wrapped up in the process
— all those lovely rules, paperwork, power plays, office politics and
other daily distractions — that the goal is forgotten or put off
indefinitely, and the new goal becomes the never-ending expansion of
the process.

I call this "Barney Fife Syndrome." If you remember the old *Andy
Griffith Show,* you'll recall that Barney loved being a sheriff's deputy,
but the last thing he wanted to do was to risk life and limb arresting an

actual criminal, which should have been his obvious job goal. And so Barney busied himself with polishing the bullet in his pocket, sweeping out the jail, and hectoring Floyd the barber about obscure ordinances. But Barney isn't the only law enforcement officer susceptible to the allure of distraction and the feeling of power that comes from being a rigid, unbending stickler for the rules. Here are a couple of examples involving real-life Barney Fifes...

• In Lakeland, Ohio, a community college student with multiple sclerosis had a car license plate that identified her as disabled. One day, she returned from class to find she had been given a ticket for *not* parking in a handicapped space. The ticket included a stern warning that if she, as a handicapped person, parked in a regular space again, her car would be towed. The overzealous police officer was reprimanded and presumably now sports a "mentally disabled" sticker on his police car.

• Some residents of Compton, California, called police to report a dead man in the front seat of a parked car, shot through the head. Police found the car and the bloody corpse — along with a parking ticket placed on the windshield by a traffic cop. The time on the ticket revealed that the cop had written it *after* passers-by had first reported that the driver was slumped dead over the steering wheel in plain sight.

While it is nice to see that the Compton Police can recognize a driver whose meter has expired, this officer was so concerned with the minutiae of his job (handing out parking tickets) that he had lost sight of the policeman's larger goal (to protect citizens from getting their brains blown out. Or at least, to notice when it happens.)

Of course, police officers are not the only professionals prone to letting piddling details and petty rules obscure their larger purpose. This is a common occurrence in any big bureaucratic organization, as noted by Dr. Laurence J. Peter of *Peter Principle* fame, who observed that all bureaucracies start out with the goal of serving the customer, but those that grow large enough eventually shift their goal from serving the customer to preserving the bureaucracy. If you've ever tried to return an item to a department store and been rebuffed with the explanation that making the customer happy is "against company policy," then you've experienced this firsthand.

For a change of pace, allow me to offer a story from my own corporate experience to illustrate how big organizations get so bogged down in the process that their goal is completely lost.

Years ago, I was hired as the writer for a pilot program at the headquarters of one of the world's leading telecommunications companies. My duties quickly expanded, and I soon found myself writing all the materials for the marketing department that would be seen by the general public: direct mail ads, informational pamphlets, surveys, etc. I was the only one there who knew how to do it, and it kept me busy from morning to night.

One day, my boss called me into her office and told me that corporate had decided to kill the original program that hired me, so my job was being eliminated. But they liked my work and wanted me to stay with the company, so she was prepared to offer me a job as a marketing analyst, at a raise in salary.

I probably should have said, "Thanks," but I was a bit taken aback, considering I had no schooling or experience as a marketing analyst, and had always found the field to be about as appealing to me, personally, as studying bovine proctology. So instead of accepting, I replied, "But I'm not a marketing analyst."

She said, "That's okay, the company will pay to train you to become a marketing analyst."

Again, I probably should've said "Thank you," but instead I asked, "Do you really *need* another marketing analyst that badly?"

"No, we have dozens."

"Well," I said, "since I'm the only one who can do what I do, and you have enough money to pay another marketing analyst you don't need, why don't you just keep me in this job and pay me out of the marketing budget?"

"No, that's impossible."

"Why?"

"Well," she explained, according to *company policy,* that would require creating a new job title for me. To do that, they were obligated to pay Arthur Andersen (a company originally created to insure that other people's books were accurate — talk about losing sight of the goal!) $80,000 to conduct a six-month feasibility study to determine if the job was needed; what the duties, pay and job title should be; and where it should fall in the corporate organizational chart.

I replied, "Well, we know the job is needed, because I'm doing it now. We know what my duties are and what my pay is. Since you're my boss, I obviously fall under you in the organizational chart. And I don't care about the title. So why do we need an $80,000, six-month feasibility study?"

"That's just the way it's done. Now, do you want to be a marketing analyst or not?"

Here we have a perfect example of a corporation in which following corporate policy has become far more important than getting the work done. From their point of view, it actually seemed wiser and more cost-effective to pay to train me to do a job they didn't need to have done at a higher salary than to let me keep doing a job they *did* need to have done, at a lower salary.

Luckily for them, once again, I quickly cut through all the confusion like a laser beam and solved their problem for them. I quit.

Another place where people often lose sight of the goal is government, where being able to stymie and confuse tax-payers with a mastery of arcane, pointless rigmarole is the key to a lifetime of job security. After all, if a problem ever really got solved, then we could fire all the bureaucrats who were allegedly "working on it." So the new goal of these workers becomes to look busy while never actually accomplishing anything (and of course, their eternal failure to accomplish the goal is always cited as proof that they need a bigger budget every year).

At the lowest strata of government, such human speed bumps are called "civil servants," while those who attain the highest level of useless, obstructionist pettifoggery are usually referred to as "The Distinguished Senator."

And how do these professional problem-solvers go about not solving a problem, or better yet, making it worse? Naturally, by becoming such rigid, unbending sticklers for their own self-created rules that enforcement of those rules begins to take precedence over the goal of solving the problem they were originally hired to fix. Here is one of my favorite examples:

Anyone who's ever visited New York City is painfully aware of the desperate shortage of public restrooms, which leaves many tourists hopping mad, or at least, hopping. Seeing a "golden opportunity," a European company installed six new self-cleaning pay toilets on Manhattan streets. Not surprisingly, they proved to be extremely popular. Their urinals were standing room only. Now, can you guess how long they lasted?

Two weeks. That's how long it took city sanitation bureaucrats to come swooping in and insist that each toilet required permits from 13 separate agencies, a waiver of a 1975 law banning pay toilets, and a complete environmental impact study. The officials said all the red tape could conceivably be rushed through in as little as two years — truly a long time to hold it in.

Now, consider that all these agencies were created with the specific goal of protecting the health, cleanliness and environment of New York — yet by rigidly enforcing every rule at their command, they managed to leave New Yorkers no alternative but to return to the healthy, clean, environmentally sound habit of relieving themselves in the alleys.

As you might imagine, this is hardly the only example of overzealous government bureaucrats losing sight of their goal...

> • An official at the Virginia Health Department, whose goal is to insure sanitary food, ordered the Roanoke Rescue Mission to stop serving deer meat donated by hunters because it wasn't state-inspected — even though the venison had been served at the Mission for 45 years without any health problems, and the only alternative for the homeless clientele was to eat garbage from Dumpsters. The state reversed the ruling, blaming a "bureaucratic mix-up." I suspect the mix-up was that someone mistakenly appointed a deer to the Health Department.

> • Jail officials in Cook County, Illinois, would normally be sticklers for following rules, but even they refused to obey the new fire code. It required all public buildings to have doors that automatically opened when the smoke alarms went off. The fire officials who wrote the code started with an admirable goal of promoting fire safety, and ended up with a set of rules that would have encouraged all prison inmates to become arsonists and set fires every day so that all the jail doors would open. If the jailers had complied with the fire code, they eventually would have had no choice but to remove the batteries from all the smoke alarms.

> • Speaking of fires, at Oregon's Malheur National Wildlife Refuge, forest rangers whose main goal is to

protect trees and wildlife devised a theory in their abundant spare time that worms emerge sooner from land that's been burned. To test it, they started a small fire. It spread out of control and burned 900 acres before it could be put out. Luckily, there were no injuries — except to a lot of trees and wildlife.

• The town council of Burgess Hill, England, had a problem: sunlight was shining through the windows of the tourism office onto some computer screens. Following standard procedures and rules, they called for bids from contractors to solve it. The contractors suggested an array of possible solutions, ranging from treating the glass with solar-reflective film to installing computer-controlled window screens. The costs ranged from about $450 to $11,000. After three meetings, six months of discussions and the creation of a six-page report, the council finally settled on the least expensive solution: they moved the computers away from the windows. Although I suspect there were some council members who would have preferred to remodel the building to move the windows away from the computers.

• The Narcotics Minister of Pakistan wanted to make a point about the dangers of drug abuse, so he held a ceremony attended by a large crowd in which he personally destroyed a mountain of illegal drugs seized by police, including 319,000 pounds of hashish. He disposed of it by putting a torch to it and burning it. After breathing in his inspiring words, the crowd went out and disposed of a mountain of Twinkies.

• A little boy in Chile was officially a girl, thanks to intractable bureaucrats. A midwife mistakenly wrote "girl" on his birth certificate. Eight years later, the government was still refusing to change it. The boy's parents feared he would suffer psychological damage and offered to let their son strip in front of a court-appointed doctor. But a spokesman for the Civil Registry, whose goal is allegedly to keep accurate records, declared that if the birth certificate said it was a girl, "then it's a girl. It doesn't make a blind bit of difference to us if the kid's got a boy's name." Or a penis, apparently. It would've been easier just to change his name to Caitlyn.

Finally, in the interest of fair play, here is an anecdote for anyone who believes private charities are always more efficient than government...

• Connecticut authorities sued a charity organization that had raised over $155,000 to fight brain tumors, claiming that only $5,000 actually went to medical research. The charity's managers allegedly spent all the rest on phone bills, fancy office furniture, flowers, luncheons, two polo matches, and round-trip airfare to fly Queen Elizabeth II's milliner to the US to judge a ladies' hat contest. They apparently believed no American could possibly have better taste in hats than the person who makes those purple velour beehives Queen Elizabeth wears. That at least proves that they were intimately familiar with brain dysfunction.

Those folks were having great fun with all the sidelights of running a charity, from impressive offices to phone calls to fundraising events. They just got so caught up in the glamour and gaiety of the brain tumor game that they lost sight of their goal, which was occasionally to pass along a few bucks to the brain researchers.

Naturally, you don't have to be wrapped up in a large organization to lose sight of your goals. Some people can accomplish this all by themselves quite nicely...

• A 19-year-old man in Catalina, Transylvania, was despondent when his fiancée dumped him for cheating on her — in itself, a fairly counterproductive act if his goal was to marry her. But then he hit on a plan to win her back by performing a marathon serenade. Planting himself beneath her bedroom window, he proceeded to sing non-stop. She repeatedly came to the window to tell him to shut up and go away, but he had forgotten that the goal was to win her back, not to set a new world serenading record. He sang on and on for 60 hours straight until neighbors finally sicced the police on him. He never persuaded his fiancée to regret dumping him, but she was awfully sorry she ever gave him that damn karaoke machine.

• A father in Vestavia Hills, Alabama, made national news by suing the school district because his teenage daughter didn't make the cheerleading squad. He claimed that the cheerleading judges discriminated against her, deprived her of due process and equal protection, violated her Fifth and Fourteenth Amendment rights, and subjected her to public humiliation and mental anguish. If his goal was to save his daughter from public humiliation and mental anguish, this was certainly a unique way to go about it.

• An ambulance driver in Houston, Texas, was fired for stopping at the drive-through window of a donut shop while taking a boy with a leg injury to the hospital. He argued that it was okay to do this because the leg injury wasn't life-threatening. But I assume the lack of donuts was.

• The North Carolina State University Women's Center wanted to raise awareness of violence against women, so they sponsored a performance of *The Vagina Monologues*. The Center's director hit on a clever scheme to promote it by selling chocolate lollipops shaped like vaginas, but the lollipops angered and offended so many female students, the controversy was the only thing reporters wanted to write about (ironically, there were no reported complaints from male students). The director complained that her noble goal of protecting women had gotten completely overshadowed by all the brouhaha over "the vagina suckers." She never imagined that women would complain about vagina suckers.

So, the moral of this chapter…

Don't lose sight of your goal, or you, too, may end up as a sucker of some sort.

HALLMARK #3: DON'T SWEAT THE DETAILS

By now, you might be spooked into developing a plan and keeping your eye on the goal. But never fear, you can still attain a coveted spot in the Loser Hall of Fame. Just make the easiest and most popular mistake of all: "Don't sweat the details."

In the overly-caffeinated world in which we live, few people have the patience for intricate details that marked the craftsmen of yesteryear. For instance, I would like to be able to paint beautiful landscapes, like the ones that Bob "Happy Little Clouds" Ross took a full 27 minutes to produce on his PBS art show. Sadly, I lack the patience to painstakingly add in every minute detail, from the fluffy white foam on the happy little waves to the red checkered kerchief on the happy little farm dog. At some point, I get tired of all that detail work and just start throwing paint at the canvas. As a result of this personal weakness, my paintings never resemble the beautiful Bob Ross landscapes on PBS. Instead, they look like the ugly Jackson Pollack monstrosities hanging at the Met.

If that doesn't scare you into paying more attention to details, I have plenty more examples, beginning with our old friends, the idiot criminals...

• Life imitated a Woody Allen movie at Il Cardinale restaurant in Germany when a gang of robbers suddenly burst through the floor with crowbars. The puzzled thieves looked around at the startled diners, realized where they were, then ran off before police arrived. They had meant to tunnel into the perfume store next door, but took a slight wrong turn and ended up under the Italian restaurant by mistake. Either they were undone by a tiny navigation detail, or they mistook the smell of ravioli for Chanel #5.

• A Hastings, Nebraska, man was arrested after he allegedly stole a snow plow, drove it to a store, and bought a case of beer. Police said he made it easy for them to track him because he used his own personal check to pay for the beer and to gas up the stolen snow plow. He was also easy to track because he was driving a *snow plow*.

• Two masked robbers burst into Chicago's Shedd Aquarium, ordered the employees to the floor, grabbed the cash, sprayed pepper spray and fled. But they were easily identified because the victims noticed that one robber's voice sounded just like that of an employee who had clocked out minutes before the robbery. Coincidentally, he was also wearing the same clothes the employee had on all day. To his credit, he did remember to take off his name tag.

• Tallahassee, Florida, police arrested two men for stealing a pair of TV sets from a home. A neighbor saw them loading the sets into their car, but they would have had time to escape if they hadn't gone back into the house. They confessed to police that they returned because they realized they'd forgotten to steal the TV remote controls. As every man knows, without the remotes, TVs are worthless.

• A 25-year-old man in Romania was released from prison after a four-year term and wanted to celebrate with a marathon sex session. He had heard that petroleum jelly was good for sex but didn't know how or why. Rather than asking someone, he simply injected his penis with six syringes full of petroleum jelly. It did swell in size, but then he collapsed in pain and was hospitalized. The fact that he had no idea how to use a sexual lubricant should tell you just how rough Romanian prisons are.

• At age 18, former child actor Brad Renfro, who starred in John Grisham's *The Client,* was arrested in Florida on grand theft charges. Police said he and an accomplice tried to steal a 45-foot yacht but overlooked the tiny detail of untying it from the dock first. It was yanked back, causing major stern damage and proving that Renfro was a young man in desperate need of a stern lecture. The cops said Renfro kept demanding, "Don't you know who I am?" Of course, they did: he was famous for playing a kid who really needed a lawyer.

• A 19-year-old night clerk at a Shawnee, Kansas, convenience store was accused of trying to fake a robbery to cover his own theft. Police said he put tape over the lenses of the store's two security cameras, then stashed the money in a trash bin and called the police to report that he'd been robbed. But he overlooked one minor detail: he had covered the camera lenses with transparent tape. What we learn from this is, for every important job, use duct tape.

• A convicted burglar escaped from a work crew in a remote part of Oklahoma by stealing a Corrections Department van. But he overlooked one detail: he didn't know where he was heading. After driving aimlessly through desolate landscape for hours, he finally stopped at a Kansas convenience store and called to ask authorities to come get him because he was hopelessly lost. He could have asked the convenience store clerk for directions, but being a man, he would rather go to prison.

Sometimes, it is not the criminal who doesn't sweat the details, but his victim, which makes him an incredibly easy mark...

• A Romanian lawyer and his accomplice were arrested for allegedly selling a businessman one-third of a building in Bucharest that they didn't own. The buyer paid about $5 million for the property, but never bothered to check any of the deeds or blueprints, which the sellers had merely photocopied from the library. The businessman showed up at his new luxury home and told the guard he had just bought it. The guard gave him a quizzical look and said, "You bought the American Embassy?" So it really *was* a bargain!

Just for a twist, here is what happens when someone who doesn't sweat the details crosses paths with a rigid stickler for the rules, as in Chapter 2...

• A would-be robber entered the Stadtsparkasse Bank in Feldmoching, Germany, went to the only empty cashier's window, pulled out a pistol and demanded money. But the staff ignored him because he was standing at the wrong window. He kept shouting, and they kept ignoring him. He eventually fled empty-handed, loudly complaining about the appalling service. He probably told them that he would *never* rob that bank again, and would advise all his friends to do the same.

As you can see, overlooking a tiny detail can spell disaster for criminals. But again, most criminals are not that intelligent to begin with. That's why so many of them are in prison, rather than living in their own palatial secret lairs in hollowed-out volcanoes, like Ernst Blofeld, Dr. Evil and Ross Perot.

So let us try an experiment. From criminals, we will gradually work our way up the I.Q. ladder to see if anyone is too smart to be immune to the temptation of not sweating the details. Next up:

average, law-abiding folk like your grandpa, your neighbors, your secretary, or the clerk down at Dairy Queen...

• A grandfather from Salatrucel, Romania, went to the drug store to buy a pacifier for his grandson, but they were out. So he bought a condom instead. He said he wasn't sure what it was, but it was rubber and it looked like a pacifier, so he thought it would comfort his grandson. Instead of praising his initiative, his furious daughter-in-law hit him in the head with a frying pan. He had to be patched up by a doctor, proving that condoms really don't protect your health all that well.

• A group of villagers in Devon, England, worked for two years to obtain a $103,000 (US) government grant to build a state-of-the-art bowling green and pavilion. They even formed a lawn bowling club, and 37 people joined. It was only then that they realized nobody in town knew how to play the game. Town officials had surveyed residents to ask what sport young and old could play together, and lawn bowling was the top answer, but it turned out nobody had actually played it. The bowling club had to take an intensive crash course in how to lawn bowl. It was only then that they realized they hated it.

• In San Antonio, Texas, some politically-correct parents were so bent on erasing any mention of the Confederacy from public buildings that they insisted the school board change the name of Jefferson Davis Middle School to "S.J. Davis Middle School," in honor of a deceased African-American school board trustee. Only after the name was changed did they learn from Davis' widow that the "S.J." stood for "Stonewall Jackson." And S.J. Davis couldn't change his own name because it was already carved in stone.

• A man in Focsani, Romania, bought two necklaces: one for his wife and one for his mistress. But he got the packages mixed up and mistakenly gave his wife the necklace with his mistress's initials on it. After she opened it, he tried to flee, but was knocked unconscious by a hurled ashtray. He was taken to a hospital, and his wife filed for divorce. This sort of thing can easily be prevented either by using name tags or by only taking mistresses who have the same initials as your wife.

• A doctor in Antwerp, Belgium, sued his own secretary for being so careless about details, she put him out of business. She threw away documents he needed for his taxes, and the fines bankrupted him. A judge ordered her to pay him $27,700 (US) in restitution. Plus a $50 refund for the flowers he gave her on Secretary's Day.

• South Wales suffered a wave of citizen attacks on suspected child molesters, but the vigilantes did not seem very concerned about details. One woman doctor was driven from her home after the vigilantes scrawled "Pedo" and various threats on her office walls. She had no history of child molestation, but the sign on her office read "Pediatrician." The vigilantes apparently didn't read it very closely and mistook it for "pedophile." I suppose she's lucky her name wasn't "Mo Lester."

• During the 2000 U.S. Presidential election, someone bought $2.12 worth of food at a Danville, Kentucky, Dairy Queen with a phony $200 bill and drove away with $197.88 change. Police said the culprit could not be charged with counterfeiting because the bill was so obviously bogus. The clerk hadn't noticed that not only is there no such thing as a $200 bill, but this particular bill had George W. Bush's face on it, the front read "The Right to Bear Arms," and the back showed the White House with oil wells on the lawn. That made it legal tender at Texas Dairy Queens only.

Okay, so maybe addled seniors, British twits and minimum wage workers aren't smart enough to pay close attention to details. But what about people who run multi-million dollar corporations whose success hinges on the safety and reliability of their products?...

• The Master Lock Company of Milwaukee voluntarily recalled 752,000 gun trigger locks and offered free replacements because the two halves could be manually separated without a key. This should hardly have surprised consumers, since the Chinese-made trigger locks actually came with a sticker reading, "Warning: Do not use on a loaded gun." They must have been targeting the niche market of extremely cautious people who put trigger locks on unloaded guns.

• The French rail company Connex spent nearly $1 million on new uniforms for its 3,000 workers, but to save time, they just guessed at their sizes. Staffers said their bosses must have thought they were all fashion models, since even short, stocky conductors received uniforms made for people who were 6-foot-2 and rail-thin. Connex was forced to replace all the uniforms, although replacing all the workers with fashion models probably would have been far better for business.

All right, so MBAs and CEOs can't be trusted with details, either. But what about those we entrust with running our governments? They handle billions of records and enforce millions of confusing laws every day. Surely, they must understand the importance of sweating the details, right?...

• Tax officials in Wexford, Pennsylvania, assessed Matt Rodriguez's property, and from their description, it sounded quite impressive. They found it to be a two-story, 10-room home with 3 ½ baths, two fireplaces, a full basement and central heat and air. In reality, it had none of those amenities because it was a 15-square-foot "fort" that Matt, who was eight years old, built himself from scrap wood. The county valued his fort at $234,300, which is still far less than the Pentagon would've paid for it.

• Taking a cue from US Postal workers who shoot anything that moves, the German Post Office began sending greeting cards to anyone who moves. But the PR stunt backfired and sparked ridicule when they sent a card to a man in Lueneburg. It wished him good luck in his new home and read, "You've made it - and now you have earned a rest so you can get used to your new surroundings." He had moved because he had to go to prison. On the bright side, they won't have to send him another moving card for 10 to 20 years.

• Transit authorities in Merseyside, England, paid $10 million (US) for a fleet of 70 new buses. It was only when a bus driver tried to take the first one on its maiden trip through the Liverpool to Birkenhead tunnel that they discovered the buses were exactly one-and-a-half inches wider than the space between the toll booths. The bus driver had to make an eight-mile detour because the buses were too fat to fit through the toll plaza. And the driver was probably too fat to fit through the tunnel.

• The Los Angeles County Department of Beaches and Harbors sold ad space on lifeguard towers and beach trash cans for posters promoting a new DVD without bothering to find out what it was. It was *Jaws*. L.A. beachgoers were suddenly surrounded by hundreds of posters of a man-eating shark. Children were crying in terror, and even adults were afraid to set foot in the ocean. The bureaucrats tried to regain the public's confidence by assuring them it was safe to go back in the water, but of course, that was exactly what the bureaucrats said in *Jaws*.

• The U.S. Naval Academy spent four years and $2.9 million planning and building a World War II memorial, but obviously didn't spend a penny on proofreaders. The plaques contained several glaring errors: Okinawa was confused with Iwo Jima, the date of Japan's surrender was off by four days, and President Roosevelt's famous line about Pearl Harbor was misquoted as a "day which will live in infamy" instead of "a date." I suppose we should be grateful it was attributed to Franklin Roosevelt and not Teddy Roosevelt.

If not even our leaders are smart enough to pay attention to the details, let's try moving still higher on the evolutionary scale, into the world of science and academia, to the pointy-headed Poindexters and effete intellectual snobs who run our schools and go to work in lab coats and are actually in charge of teaching the rest of us how to think. These highly-degreed brainiacs would never be caught doing something so mundane as goofing off and screwing up important details, would they? I ask you: *would* they?!...

• A group of top British government scientists was assigned the task of assessing the dangers of mad cow disease to the nation's sheep flock. After four years of experiments on a "soup of homogenized sheep brains," they made a startling discovery: due to a labeling error, they had been mistakenly testing cow brains instead. Apparently, the "soup of homogenized sheep brains" had been mistakenly sent to Scotland for a Christmas dinner.

• Washington, DC, education officials paid $41,000 to put banner ads on 75 buses. The ads read, "DC Public Schools Wants You. Go to Class! It' A Blast!" School officials blamed the printer for the typos, but school superintendent Paul Vance fumed that it was "absolutely inexcusable." He said, "It reinforces the perception that we're less than competent!" Especially since that printer probably graduated from a DC public school.

• School history textbooks have become so riddled with factual errors, political correctness and revisionism that they now provide fulltime employment for dozens of self-appointed textbook watchdogs. One American history book came in for heavy criticism because it devoted more space to Marilyn Monroe than to George Washington, even though it is undeniable that Marilyn would have looked a lot hotter coming across on the Delaware.

• One would think that a lifetime of mixing volatile chemicals in beakers would instill a respect for getting details right, but not even science textbook writers are immune to the plague of sloppiness. A North Carolina State University study of twelve of America's most popular science texts turned up over 500 pages of glaring errors. The books misstated Newton's First Law of Physics, showed the Equator passing through the southern United States, and featured a photo of Linda Ronstadt labeled as "a silicon crystal." That caption was supposed to go under a photo of Pamela Anderson.

The point is that no matter how smart or professional you may be, it is still very easy to overlook some tiny detail that can snowball into an embarrassing disaster. Remember that the most carefully-laid plans of man can be derailed by something so tiny as to be microscopic. The gonorrhea microbe, for example. So pay attention to the details. Measure twice and cut once, check and double-check your work, and never publish your writings without meticulously proofreading them first.

And now, let's move on to Hallmark #3.

HALLMARK #4: DON'T COMMUNICATE CLEARLY

I have a Magna Cum Laude degree in Communications. This qualifies me to do two things:

1. Fry Whoppers

2. Talk about communications.

So you can trust me when I tell you this: Communicating clearly is very important.

Very, *very* important.

Got it? Good. Then all that college tuition was worth it.

The key to proper communications can be summed up in one word: "KISS." By this, I mean "Keep It Simple, Stupid," and not that you should dress like Gene Simmons. However, KISS is a good example of the concept. They kept their songs both simple and stupid, and outlasted many bands with far more talent. When your lyrics consist of the phrase, "I want to rock and roll all night and party every day" repeated 249 times, it is very hard for your audience to misinterpret your meaning.

You may think you communicate so clearly that you could not possibly be misunderstood, but beware: you are just one slip of the tongue away from opening up a shipment of alligator pears to discover that you've ordered a pair of alligators instead. In fact, poor communications skills can even land you in jail...

- A lawyer in Montgomery, Alabama, was defending a young man accused of drug possession. To communicate his contention that the prosecutor was keeping jurors "in the dark" by withholding information, he started flipping the light switch in the courtroom on and off. His attempted dramatics backfired when the judge sent him to jail for contempt. He's probably lucky his client didn't start shouting, "Whoa! I'm havin' a flashback!"

The most basic type of miscommunication comes when someone in a foreign nation attempts a bad translation of a sign or appliance manual into English. Humorous examples constantly pop up in your e-mail, and many are likely apocryphal so I won't bothering quoting them. (Oh, all right, I'll quote one. "Sign in a Hong Kong hotel room: 'Drop your trousers here if you wish our maids to service you.'")

Again, anyone who is writing a hand-lettered sign in an unfamiliar language can make simple translation errors, but it takes a special kind of incompetence to make a costly and embarrassing faux pas when you are part of a large group of corporate professionals assigned the task of communicating with a foreign language market. Yet with enough diligence, it can be done...

• Sky Harbor International Airport in Phoenix, Arizona, posted bilingual signs to greet Spanish-speaking visitors. One sign literally read, "Violators will be deceased." Another said that to drink legally in Arizona, you must have "21 anuses." This was supposed to read "You must be 21 years old," although to be fair, some people returning from Mexico feel as if they *do* have 21 anuses.

• Those wishing to count the anuses of Spanish-speaking tourists would have done well to stake out the Braniff terminal in 1987. The airline ran radio commercials in Spanish touting their comfy leather seats but didn't realize that the phrase "en cuero" ("in leather"), when spoken aloud, sounds like "en cueros" ("naked"). Worse, the TV version that extolled the three extra inches of leg room promised that passengers would fly "en cuero con tres pulgadas mas," which sounded as if they were bragging Braniff's passengers "fly naked with three inches more." I shudder to think how they might have mistranslated Braniff's previous slogan, "We really move our tails for you."

• Detroit automakers love to give cars evocative names that often lose something in the translation. One famous example is when Chevrolet had difficulty selling the Nova in South America until they finally figured out that "no va" is Spanish for "doesn't go." A less well-known but even more embarrassing cultural clash blindsided Ford when they attempted to market the Pinto in Brazil, only to learn that "pinto" is a Brazilian slang term for "small male genitals." But then, that's pretty much what driving a Pinto implies in America, too.

• Coca-Cola found it particularly hard to crack the Chinese market. First, they had to change the product's name after they discovered that the Chinese phonetic equivalent of "Co-ca-Co-la" translated to the rather unappetizing "Bite the wax tadpole." Sales were next stymied when the slogan "Coke Adds Life" was translated into Chinese as "Coke Brings Your Dead Ancestors Back To Life," and China already had enough of an overpopulation problem.

• Not to be outdone in the Cola Wars, Pepsi also laid claim to the ability to reanimate the dead, when their slogan "Come Alive!" was translated into German as "Rise from the grave!"

• Still, it's no surprise that both Coke and Pepsi were more popular than Coors Beer in Spain, at least until Coors realized that their slogan "Turn It Loose" translated into a Spanish colloquialism for "Get Diarrhea," which might have been a more appropriate slogan for Taco Bell.

Of course, it is hardly necessary to tackle an unfamiliar language to make yourself completely misunderstood. Many people manage it quite nicely in their own native tongue, usually by relying too heavily on the greatest enemy of clear communication: *jargon.*

Jargon has been spreading like kudzu over the past 20 years or so, to the point that it has spilled out of the boardrooms, courtrooms and capitol domes to infest every corner of American life, turning the simplest statements into baffling mazes of overinflated verbiage. Thanks to jargon, it no longer rains at the trailer park. Instead, there is a precipitation event at the mobile home lifestyle center.

During my time as a writer for the corporate world, I was often called upon to take jargon-filled speeches written by executives and translate them into English so the workers could understand them. It always amazed me that a company was able to function at all when its leaders were so incapable of communicating with the workers that it would have taken them a three-page memo to yell "Fire!" So let me give you this tip:

> *If you want to be a successful manager, become bilingual. Learn your industry's gobbledygook well enough to be recognized as executive material, but don't forget how to speak plain English so you can still communicate with your employees without having to hire someone like me to translate for you.*

Every industry from medicine to the Internet has its own buzz words that are incomprehensible to outsiders, but the true masters of jargon are able to trowel it on so thickly that even their own colleagues can't make heads or tails out of it. For some lovely examples of truly world-class impenetrable jargon, let us turn to the Plain English Campaign, an organization formed in Great Britain to promote clear language and to fight the jargon epidemic. (And take just a moment to ponder how bad the problem must be when English people have to remind other English people to speak English.)

Each year, the Plain English Campaign hands out its Golden Bull Awards for the most horribly botched attempts at communication. Some of the winners for the year 2000 were as funny as they were eye-crossing...

• Here is how the Luton, England, Education Authority described its program that teaches poor kids how to drive go-carts: It's "a multi-agency project catering for holistic diversionary provision to young people for positive action linked to the community safety strategy and the pupil referral unit." *Whee!*

• The South West of England Regional Development Agency issued a leaflet reading, "Aligning the Drivers, Values and Principles with the Objectives is the key to unlocking the strategy. When they are fully aligned, they will illuminate the actions that need to be taken..." This either explained the agency's mission or revealed how to unlock the Gates of Hades and begin the Apocalypse, it's not clear which.

• The Britannia Building Society offered this simple, one-sentence definition of a "Special Resolution" to replace an earlier definition that wasn't clear enough:

A Special Resolution, "in relation to a resolution proposed or to be proposed, means any resolution that the Statutes or these Rules require to be passed as a Special Resolution if it is to be effective for its purpose or which is a resolution (not being a

resolution which if passed would purport to
interfere with the Directors' right and duty to
manage the affairs of the Society) which is
specified in a Members' requisition referred to in
Rule 31 (3) (a) or in a Members' Notice referred to
in Rule 33 (1) (c) and which as its only or main
object or consequence or as one of its main objects
or consequences seeks that the Board consider,
investigate, effect or supply information in relation
to a transfer of the Society's business to a
commercial company or a merger with another
building society or a dissolution or winding up of
the Society."

We can only imagine what the earlier, unclear definition
was like.

But now, let us leave our friends in the UK (who, after all, are
British, so we don't expect them to speak understandable English) and
turn our attention to some good old-fashioned, American-made
gibberish.

When you think of confusing gobbledygook, naturally, you think
first of lawyers. There is now a movement underway to replace
legalese with plain language, but it's an uphill battle, as evidenced by
the "Legaldegook Awards" presented each year by the State Bar of
Texas for the absolute worst in legal writing. A few proud winners...

   • The "Fogginess Award" went to a legal brief which
   began   with   this: "Non-contingent,   conceptual,
   semantic connectedness is an absolutely necessary
   condition for sameness of meaning." Well, obviously.

   • The "Tongue Twister" award was presented to a new
   state law on the "Shucking of Shellfish," which read, in
   part, "Only safe and wholesome shellfish shall be

shucked." Shucked from their sea shells by the seashore, of course.

• Finally, brace yourself for this one. Here, in its entirety, is the winner of the "Uninviting Invitation Award for the Invitation Least Likely to Be Accepted Gleefully":

"Pursuant to the aforesaid, I would now sincerely request that you consider the within correspondence as a formal invitation to make an appearance so as to advise of your expertise and the various day-to-day procedures involving same.

In addition to the aforesaid, we might have numerous attendees. Accordingly, I would now respectfully request your consideration with respect to an appearance and ask that your assistant establish contact with my office so that arrangements can be made at a time convenient with your schedule.

I now thank you for your sincere attention to the above and shall await your response as relevant to the same."

Well, when they put it that way, who can say no?

Another rich vein of linguistic fool's gold runs through America's universities, where the political correctness movement has insured that any words with actual meanings have been banned and replaced with words that can't offend anyone because nobody knows what the heck they mean. Every year, the Young America Foundation releases its "Dirty Dozen" list of the twelve most absurdly P.C. college classes in the US, all of which must be prerequisites for a BS degree. Here are a few honorees, taken verbatim from the course descriptions, to show you what your kids are getting for your $30,000-a-year tuition payments...

• Villanova University's "Eco Feminism" class promises to explore "the role of eco-feminist thought in the development of a 'postmodern' societal paradigm."

• The University of California-Irvine's "Sexism and Power" course teaches that "males and females are objects constructed in powered language dominated and controlled by males to their positional and distributional advantage."

• And of course, the windiest of all comes from venerable Harvard, where the "Multicultural Biblical Criticism" course threatens to examine how "ethnicity, feminist, womanish, black, queer, liberation theological, postcolonial, and Third World studies have begun to de-center the hegemonies paradigm of biblical studies."

Thus answering the question, "Why do college students binge drink?"

To sum up, if you want to be understood, keep your message and your language as simple as possible. Remember what author Olin Miller said:

"The person who uses a lot of big words isn't trying to inform you; he's trying to impress you."

Or to phrase it more succinctly: "Postmodern male and/or female personages who utilize a hyperextended linguistic bloviation paradigm seek not to impart a meaning vector but to achieve through semantic disconnectedness a hegemonistic positional superiority."

I hope that clears it up for you.

HALLMARK #5: WORK WHILE DRUNK, HIGH OR OTHERWISE INDULGING YOUR ADDICTIONS

It should go without saying that becoming addicted to alcohol, drugs or tobacco is not the best route to career success, unless you want to become a dead rock star and make the cover of Rolling Stone. For most people, being stoned or drunk is a major impediment to achieving peak efficiency. For instance, would this book be as good had I chugged Jack Daniels and licked LSD tabs while writing it? No. It would have even more misspellings. On the plus side, people might mistake it for a lost Hunter S. Thompson book, and it would sell a lot more copies.

In our touchy-feely "12-Step" culture, we are constantly being told that everyone deserves an unlimited number of second chances. Even after his umpteenth drug charge, but before his famous comeback, Robert Downey Jr. was offered a regular role on *Ally McBeal,* where he was actually the cast member who looked the least like an emaciated junkie. But Robert Downey Jr. was the rare consummate professional dopehead, a unique talent who could turn in Emmy-worthy performances even while hallucinating that his leading lady was a giant talking banana. While your run-of-the-mill substance abuser might think he is fooling the world, it is quite unusual to find anyone who can accomplish much of substance while taking a mental magic carpet ride to Candyland...

• A 32-year-old heroin addict broke into the Princess Diana Retirement Home in Newcastle, England, but he failed to steal anything. Two little old ladies, aged 80 and 71, caught him in their bedroom, grappled with him, shoved him into the bathroom, and kept him locked up there until police arrived.

Okay, that should give you an idea of what heroin does to your upper body strength. But what do drugs do to your mind? Well...

• A female police officer pulled into the drive-thru of a Whataburger in a Dallas, Texas, suburb and ordered a breakfast burrito. The 18-year-old cook put marijuana in her eggs, but the cop smelled the drugs before taking a bite, and the teenager was fired and arrested. A police spokesman said he'd never seen anything so stupid: there were mirrors there, so the teen knew he was handing pot to a cop, but he apparently couldn't resist because he thought it would be really funny. I bet everything seemed really funny to him.

• A 24-year-old man walked into a police station in Philadelphia and made a complaint against two men who had beaten him up during a drug deal. As police took his statement, they recognized him as the suspect in a bank robbery from ten days before and arrested him. When he robbed the bank, he had demanded all the teller's cash, When she told him she had only one dollar, he had grabbed that and fled. The drug dealers probably beat him up when he asked how much blow he could buy for a dollar.

• A U.S. Appeals Court in Arizona allowed a death row inmate a hearing to determine if the trial judge who sentenced him was stoned on marijuana. Several years later, the judge had been removed from the bench after being busted twice for pot possession. If the judge sentenced a man to death while stoned, we can only imagine what his punishments were like when he was *not* mellowed out.

• An Indianapolis man told a uniformed officer to call him if he ever wanted to sell drugs the police had confiscated. So the cop made a date to meet him. The man got into his squad car, paid $200 for 56 grams of coke, offered to pay the rest after he sold it, said "Thanks," then got out. He was arrested immediately. A police spokesman said that in 20 years on the force, it was the first time anyone ever tried to buy drugs from a uniformed police officer. You would think that someone with that few brain cells left would at least have a working knowledge of how to buy drugs.

• A 32-year-old woman was arrested by Colorado police for violating her parole on a theft and drug charge by handling guns. In an act of naked stupidity, she posed nude while holding a variety of guns and allowed the photos to be posted on the Internet. Police recognized the electronic ankle bracelet that monitored her movements because it was the only thing she was wearing. They also recognized the guns from her boyfriend's collection. And of course, they recognized her .38s.

• Customs agents at the Bogota, Colombia, airport nabbed a German tourist who was trying to smuggle out a stash of cocaine hidden in five cans of dog food. They got suspicious when he gave nervous and inconsistent answers to the question of why he needed all that dog food on a flight that didn't allow pets. If he still had brain cells, he could have simply answered, "Have you ever tasted airline food?"

• A Canton, Ohio, man was walking down the street, carrying a potted marijuana plant he had grown. At one point, he turned to a passerby and marveled, "Would you believe I'm walking down the street in the middle of the day with this pot plant?" The man replied, "Would you believe I'm a cop?" He was indeed a plainclothes officer, and he arrested the potted perambulator. Would you believe anyone could be that stupid?

As you can see, these people disprove the notion that "your brain on drugs" is like a fried egg, since a fried egg is obviously much smarter than they are.

Of course, drugs like marijuana, heroin and cocaine are hardly the only substances that one can find in Larry Loser's locker. Not only is alcohol a drug, but alcoholism is the most common (and as our society has determined, the funniest) of all major substance addictions. To prove this, try sitting through a double bill of *Arthur* and *Scarface,* and see which one has more laughs, if you don't count Al Pacino's Cuban accent.

From Falstaff to W.C. Fields to Dean Martin to Homer Simpson, pathetic drunks have always been one of our greatest sources of amusement. But why content ourselves with Hollywood's make-believe boozehounds when we are surrounded by the real thing, all making hilariously futile attempts to blend in and function normally while utterly plastered?...

> • Two 20-year-old German men got drunk at a business conference at the Frankfurt Airport and went looking for a toilet. They wandered around, ended up on the tarmac, and stumbled onto a shuttle that took them to a plane, which took off. When it landed, they noticed that they felt cold. That's because they were in Moscow, with no passports. Russian police sent them back to Frankfurt, where German police met them and arrested them for joyriding. They could argue that when you drink 15 beers, then go six hours in a freezing place without a bathroom, there is no "joy" involved.

> • In Wheeling, West Virginia, a drunken robber who was more loaded than his gun stole a rifle from a house, then stole a box of shells from Wal-Mart, then

went to a sex shop and demanded money. But when he pulled the trigger, the gun misfired because he had stolen the wrong size ammo. The clerk subdued him and held him until police arrived. Luckily, sex shop clerks are used to dealing with guys who misfire because their bullet is too small for the chamber.

• In the Australian Outback, a young man who had already been banned from driving drank three cartons of beer, then got lost driving to a local college. With his blood alcohol at eight times the legal limit, he decided to do the smart thing: he stopped at a police station to ask directions. Two officers watched him as he drove up *very* slowly, occasionally swerving off the road, then finally stopped and asked them directions to the college. He ended up in jail instead. This is why men never stop to ask directions.

• A 57-year-old drunken man attempted to walk home from a pub in Dorset, England, and fell into a harbor. A lifeboat, a helicopter and police, fire and ambulance crews all rushed out to save him, and he was sent home. Fifteen minutes later, a call came that the same drunk had made it a double and had fallen back into the same harbor again. This time, a few firemen brought a ladder and rescued him. The third time it happened, the bartender tossed him an inner tube.

• A Bradenton, Florida, teen who suffered a ruptured aorta after driving into a tree sued the police for not realizing he was drunk and arresting him before he could hurt himself. He claimed that just before the crash, a cop pulled him from his girlfriend's window, which he was trying to enter, and let him drive away despite his being obviously drunk and having a car seat covered with beer cans. At the time of the lawsuit, the cop was no longer on the force, after he admitted to having a crack cocaine habit. I assume the cop sued the police for not realizing he was on the pipe when he failed to notice the teenage drunk.

• A 45-year-old man had been drinking and fishing all day with his buddies on a creek in Viburnum, Missouri, when he suddenly shouted, "Hey, watch this!" Snatching a five-inch perch from the water, he dropped it headfirst into his mouth and began gasping for air. His friends couldn't dislodge the fish, so they called 911, but he was dead by the time medics arrived. (Tip: Anytime a drunk says, "Hey, watch this!," just go ahead and call 911 immediately.)

• At a bar in El Paso, Texas, a drunk became belligerent and was ordered to leave. As he was being escorted out, he pulled a gun. But since he wasn't thinking too clearly, he pulled out his heavy revolver using his prosthetic arm — and his arm fell off. His arm was lying on the floor with a gun in its hand. He was charged with assault and aggravated assault, but, of course, not armed assault.

• A would-be thief in Brazil broke into a church and had already bundled up a projector and a vacuum cleaner to haul away when he stumbled on the supply of Communion wine. Two bottles later, he passed out cold. He was discovered there the next morning, still sound asleep. Proving that the Lord works in mysterious ways His blunders to achieve.

• A man entered a store in Braintree, England, and asked a clerk to direct him to the pantyhose. He went to the display, pulled a pair of pantyhose over his head, then came back and robbed the same clerk. She said she suspected he was drunk because he smelled very strongly of alcohol. And he had chosen crotchless pantyhose.

• A man in Dublin, Ireland, went on a three-day bender at Christmas, then decided to rob the shop next door. He got a knife and put on a mask, but he was so drunk, as he walked to the store, he kept lifting the mask to greet passersby. His lawyer admitted he displayed a "complete lack of criminal professionalism," as well as an inability to tell Christmas from Halloween.

• In 1997, a 23-year-old man in Sydney, Australia, consumed 57 drinks in a hotel drinking game, tried to walk home over a pedestrian bridge and fell off it. So he sued the Roads and Traffic Authority for building the bridge. He couldn't remember how he fell, but he thought he'd slipped through a gap. He claimed the government was negligent for leaving a gap when they knew drunks would often be walking there. He settled the case after the judge said he could not prove he didn't just fall over the rail. Especially after he fell over the court rail.

• A man in Sibiu, Romania, was celebrating the birth of his first child when he accepted a party bet from friends. The bet must've been intended to prove that a drunken man will put his penis into anything, for it somehow required him to insert his manhood into a metal wheel bearing. It got stuck, so he reached for yet another tool and tried to cut off the wheel bearing with an electric circular saw. The saw slipped and sliced his penis off. After a five-hour reattachment operation, surgeons said he would be back to normal in a few months. Or as close to normal as a man who has drunken sex with a wheel bearing can be said to be.

Those anecdotes should serve as a lesson to anyone who has ever said to himself, "I just had one drink/snort/shot/huff/doobie/kilo, so I'm sure nobody at the office noticed anything was wrong," as his boss was calling a SWAT team and his secretary was trying to put her shredded blouse back on. Remember, drugs do not induce paranoia; they merely heighten your ability to sense that everybody else really is staring at you.

But what about other addictions? Is it safe to indulge them at work? Let's put the drugs and alcohol aside for a moment. Go on, I'll wait...okay, now that your hands are free, you are probably itching to pick up a cigarette. Well, be warned: in today's offices, smoking tobacco can be as harmful to your career as it is to your lungs, and it can get you into more trouble than smoking crack — unless you smoke your crack in your cubicle instead of in the designated outdoor crack-smoking area.

An addiction to tobacco can not only destroy your health, alienate your co-workers, make you smell like a fire sale and make kissing you as pleasant as licking out a bar ashtray, but the desperate need for a cigarette is a weakness and a distraction that can seriously undermine your ability to think clearly and achieve your goals...

> • A man in Monchengladbach, Germany, was dumped by his girlfriend and decided to end it all by turning on the gas jets in his apartment. But after awhile, he changed his mind and turned them off. Rattled by his near-death experience, he felt a nagging need for a cigarette to calm his nerves, so he lit one up. The resulting explosion blew the roof off his apartment building, but luckily, no one was injured. It was a miracle that everyone in the building didn't die from secondhand smoking.

> • A 63-year-old Romanian man who was paralyzed from the waist down was desperate for a cigarette, but he had dropped his lighter on the floor. So he called the fire department to come pick it up for him. But going without smoking had made him so nervous, he kept dropping it after they left, so he had to keep calling back. He called out the fire brigade four times

in eight hours to help him light his cigarette. One would hope that after the fourth visit, they would have thought to drop his phone on the floor.

As you can see, addictions of any kind, even to tobacco, can erode your abilities and your popularity, distract you from completing your work, and turn you into not just a loser, but a pathetic loser. Even being the boss does not make you immune. If you don't believe me, consider what happened to the most powerful boss on earth when he combined an addiction to cigars with an addiction to sex with young, large-mouthed interns.

And now, it's time to set down this book and take a brief break, because I'm sure you could use a drink and personally, I'll die if I don't have a Snickers bar.

HALLMARK #6: CALL UNDUE ATTENTION TO YOURSELF

President Ronald Reagan used to keep a sign on his desk in the Oval Office that read, "There is no limit to what a man can do or where he can go if he doesn't mind who gets the credit." I don't know who said this originally, but many people gave the credit to Reagan, and he never turned it down.

Admittedly, it is tough to take advice about not courting attention from a man whose major careers included male model, Hollywood actor and politician. Despite all that blatant attention-mongering, Ronald Reagan was certainly no loser. Likewise, Donald Trump is fabulously successful, and he is so attracted to the spotlight that he is rumored to have moth DNA. Our pop culture landscape is littered with "celebrities" whose entire careers, if one can call them that, stem from nothing but their willingness to do anything, from eating scorpions to rolling around in rats, to call attention to themselves. These people include *Fear Factor* contestants, anyone who has ever appeared on a reality show, and all known Kardashians, living or dead.

Believe it or not, there is such a thing as "bad attention." Being recognized with an award for excellence by your peers is *good* attention. For instance, if someone offers you the Nobel Prize for Physics, I suggest you take it. However, grabbing attention at the wrong time or for the wrong reasons is double-plus ungood. For instance, having people point at you as you walk down the street and shout, "Hey, it's that promiscuous, bug-eating rat-wallower from TV!" is *bad* attention.

Getting noticed is great, if you are noticed at the right moments for the right reasons. That's why celebrities hire press agents: to make sure the media take notice whenever their clients do something praiseworthy, such as dishing out Thanksgiving dinner to their former personal assistants down at the homeless shelter or graduating from rehab for the 25th time. But when that same celebrity staggers into an awards show with eyeballs as red as two cherry tomatoes, reeking of bourbon and lightly frosted with angel dust, wearing the jacket of a baby blue 1977 tux with a pair of paisley pajama bottoms and a tampon on his head, and accompanied by two half-naked porn stars, his press agent does not insist that the cameras come in for a close-up. That's Kathy Griffin's job.

No matter how tempting it may be to invite the world's notice, sometimes it's just plain counterproductive. Again, let's start with the people who should know this truism better than anyone: criminals...

• A 20-year-old Tallahassee, Florida, car thief was arrested after he illegally parked his stolen car in a handicapped space with the stereo blasting. Of course, this drew the attention of a passing cop, who simply told him to move on. But the thief rudely snapped that he was just visiting a shop and would move in a couple of minutes. That irritated the cop so much that he ran a license check, discovered the car was stolen and busted the driver, who also turned out to be carrying cocaine. The officer said, "He's not exactly a criminal mastermind." In fact, if he had been parked in a space for the mentally handicapped, the cop probably wouldn't have questioned him.

• The owner of a bridal shop in Totness, England, saw a wedding photo in the newspaper and thought something about it looked oddly familiar. Then she realized that the bride and her fiancé had been in her store acting suspicious just before one of her gowns disappeared. The bride had actually posed for the newspaper wearing the stolen gown. She was fined $300, and the groom was charged with theft. The judge didn't buy their "something borrowed" excuse.

• A Hamburg, New York, man set fire to a shop, then called a friend to brag about it. As soon as he heard "Hello?" on the other end, he blurted out, "Dude, it's lit! The whole corner is going!" But he had dialed a wrong number and mistakenly called the fire chief. He was charged with arson. Proving that dimwitted people should not play with matches or telephones.

• A thief in Singapore snatched a woman's purse, used one of her stolen credit cards to buy two mobile phones, and hurried out when he thought the store keeper was getting suspicious. However, he later decided he'd been overcharged — on the credit card that wasn't even his — went back to the same shop to complain, and made a scene. The owner called the cops. He was a lousy thief, but he was a terrific shopper.

• A thief stole a car in Melville, New York, and abandoned it months later, stripped of parts. The only thing he left behind was the owner's camera. When she had her film developed, she was stunned to discover that the thief had taken a photo of himself smiling into the camera lens, and another of the exit ramp to his neighborhood. His grinning mug appeared in all the New York City papers, beneath such appropriate captions as "The Picture of Stupidity."

• A woman in Muskegon Heights, Michigan, was allegedly shoplifting at a Family Dollar store. She set off an alarm as she left, then dropped her purse in the parking lot. She later called police to claim her lost purse and even came down to police headquarters to retrieve it. Naturally, she was arrested. But then, they figured she was dumb when she risked prison to shoplift at the *dollar store.*

• A registered sex offender wanted for walking away from a halfway house was captured in San Diego after he was noticed walking in a park, wearing an orange shirt with the word "FUGITIVE" printed on it in large block letters. A police spokesman said it was just a shirt he had and liked, so he wore it. Besides, his "REGISTERED SEX OFFENDER" T-shirt was in the wash.

• An ex-con sued the Australian prison system for $265,000, claiming that because of their confusing recordkeeping system, he'd been held 239 days longer than he should have. So prison authorities in Queensland recalculated his sentence and discovered that he was right about his release date being incorrect: he had actually been released six weeks too early. They never would have noticed if he hadn't called attention to it. He was sent back to jail for another six weeks. See, he *told* them it was confusing!

In all the above cases, the poor losers who called attention to themselves did so primarily because they were dumber than a mud lump. But stupidity is not the only underlying cause of a thirst for attention. Competent, even intelligent, crooks can also call too much attention to themselves, just through sheer arrogance...

• A man confessed to defrauding casinos and credit card companies out of more than $1 million by opening approximately 108 lines of credit under false names. He was finally captured after a bank clerk in Lubbock, Texas, noticed that he was applying for credit in the name of the Three Stooges' law firm, "Dewey, Cheatham & Howe." The clerk said it "seemed unusual for a company name," but it had fooled a lot of people. Then again, a lot of people are knuckleheads.

• A Florida fraud suspect who cashed nearly $200,000 worth of bad checks got so cocky, he made a video and sent it to the police, taunting them by saying, "Here I am, now you know what I look like! Catch me if you can!" They did. They drove over to his mother's house in Hialeah, and there he was. Turned out being a criminal genius was a lot harder than it seemed in his comic books.

• Proving that comedy is not for amateurs, a man got up at open mic night at a Macon, Georgia, comedy club and began doing "slice of life" jokes about the subject he knew best: the three bank robberies he had pulled. The audience thought it was a skit, but the club manager, an ex-cop, realized it wasn't and called the police. The would-be funnyman was captured and sentenced to a rather big slice of Life: 87 years in prison. At least he now has a captive audience for his jokes.

And so we learn that calling undue attention to yourself is a definite career drag for criminals. But what about those who crave attention as an easy way of advancing themselves? Everyone wants to be popular, and in our media-saturated society, people have lost sight of this ancient truth:

"Fame is not the same thing as popularity."

It's tempting to think that making an overt grab for attention is the first step on the road to winning your true love, advancing your favorite cause, or being the most popular person on your block. Well, dream on...

• A Hong Kong woman who was jilted by her married lover decided that the way to win him back was to be impossible to ignore. So she phoned him approximately 1,000 times a day for three years. After two years, the man quit his job and changed all his phone numbers to avoid her; but she found out his new numbers, resumed the calls and started sending him 500 faxes a day as well. She may never land another boyfriend, but she could easily land a job as a bill collector.

• The Blackpool, England, soccer team was poised to beat rival Torquay 2-1 when a Blackpool fan became so overjoyed, he stripped off his clothes and ran naked onto the field to celebrate. Play had to be stopped while the cops removed him, and four minutes were added onto the clock to compensate for the distraction. In that extra time, Torquay scored twice to win the game. That's the penalty Blackpool paid for having too many balls on the field.

• A sexy, 27-year-old animal rights activist decided to draw attention to her anti-fur crusade by standing outside a busy Tucson, Arizona, shopping center, wearing nothing but panties and a strategically-placed banner reading, "Human Skin In, Animal Skin Out." She got more attention than she bargained for when male drivers slammed on the brakes to gawk, resulting in a multi-car pile-up. All her stunt accomplished was to prove that nothing is more eye-catching than the skin of a fox.

• Members of an antique rifle club in Yorkshire, England, chose an attention-getting name: "The Cock, Ball, Nipple and Touchhole Club." Those are all parts on an antique rifle. But the gimmick backfired when the local bank closed their checking account for being just 32 pence overdrawn. A bank spokesman claimed unconvincingly that the account closure was not due to the club's filthy-sounding name. Nor to his keen disappointment after he subscribed to their newsletter.

• An Essex, England, man who was locally famous for his elaborate Christmas decorations decided to do "something a bit different" to draw even more attention. He spent $950 on a 30-foot-tall inflatable snowman with a giant top hat and a massive carrot nose. It drew crowds of strangers, but it made him very unpopular with his own neighbors. They said it seemed to be staring at them through their bedroom windows, and some complained of having nightmares about being chased by a giant snowman. He became infamous to his neighbors as the guy who brought in the abominable snowman.

Maybe drawing lots of attention to yourself isn't always the best way to advance socially. Still, there's no denying that in order to advance on the job, you must get noticed. If you don't, you may spend the rest of your career in a cubicle, dreaming of the day when you can retire and live out your last years in a tiny room that actually has a fourth wall and a ceiling.

But beware: your job is the place where the difference between "good attention" and "bad attention" becomes critical. Being noticed by your boss because you landed a million-dollar sales contract is "good attention." Being noticed by your boss because you photocopied your butt at the office Christmas party and e-mailed a copy to everyone on the board of directors is "bad attention." Unless you have an incredibly attractive butt.

As Robbie Knieval could tell you, attention-getting stunts are an extremely risky way to advance your career and can have quite the opposite effect...

• Eight stockbrokers in Toronto thought it would be good publicity to take part in a newspaper stock-picking contest. After one year, the results of their picks ranged from an 84 percent loss to a 149.3 percent gain. But they were all beaten by a ninth competitor: a wind-up toy Santa in a little helicopter whose blades came to rest pointing at a Texas oil and gas company whose stock rose 179.2 percent. In similar contests, attention-seeking brokers were humiliated by a five-year-old girl who threw darts at a financial page and a zoo orangutan that pointed at stocks at random. The brokers couldn't figure out why they lost, since these were the same methods they use to pick stocks.

• An actor in Madras, India, had the lead in a play about a real-life martyred missionary who was burned to death. Without telling his co-stars, he tried to impress the critics by using real gasoline to douse himself on stage. When another actor happened to light a match, he went up like a Roman candle. It was his final performance anywhere, but at least critics couldn't deny that it was a blazing performance that lit up the stage.

• During the big dot-com collapse of 2000, *USA Today* analyzed the spending of some failed websites and discovered that they had made the mistake of thinking that grabbing attention automatically translated into success. Thanks to cool Super Bowl ads, extravagant parties and other expensive PR gimmicks, one in six of the Internet firms still in business in 2000 needed to increase its sales tenfold just to break even. The one boo-hooing loudest was the fashion site Boo.com, which blew $223 million on ads and attracted only 550,000 customers. They could've simply bribed their customers $400 each to shop there and still saved $2.75 million. But that wouldn't have been as cool.

Some people can't even wait until they land the job before they start trying to get attention. Here's a tip for job seekers: unless you are interviewing for a job with Ringling Brothers, a job interview is not the place to demonstrate your ability to spit fireballs, turn cartwheels or juggle any three items from your interviewer's desktop. Oh, you think nobody could be *that* dumb?...

> • A job recruitment agency manager in Manchester, England, complained that either job hunters are getting stupider or else they don't understand that silly answers on applications don't get attention, they just get you rejected. The manager cited as examples a truck driver who said he could drive any type of truck, "as long as it wasn't orange"...a man who wrote that the person he gave as a reference didn't have a phone number because he's dead.... and a woman who claimed her previous job duties included "juggling, standing on my head and knitting fog." That could only have been true if she had worked for an Internet company in the late '90s.

Finally, remember that due to open cubicles, security cameras, electronic communications eavesdropping and all the other privacy-crushing aspects of modern office life, it is now quite easy to draw "bad attention" to yourself without even trying. Unless you are deliberately aiming for a career as the town dogcatcher of Loserville, then here is a rule you should always obey:

"Never pull any undignified, attention-getting stunt at work, even if you think that nobody who could fire you is watching!"

If you think that's too extreme, perhaps this final illustration will put the fear of God into you...

• A 26-year-old P.R. agent from London gave new meaning to
the term "public relations" when she sent a naughty e-mail to
her boyfriend, detailing an oral sex act she had performed on
him. He proudly forwarded it to six pals at his law firm. His
friends couldn't resist passing it on to others. Within days, the
e-mail, still bearing the woman's name and her employer's
name, spread around the world. She was suddenly inundated
with so many e-mails from horny fans, they crashed her
company's computer system. Her boyfriend's law firm took
disciplinary action against him, tabloid reporters camped on
their lawns, and the couple were forced into seclusion in their
homes until it all…ahem…"blew over."

You can bet that from now on, the only time this woman uses the
word "sucks" at work will be when she is talking about the Internet.

HALLMARK #7: LOSE YOUR COOL

The world is filled with self-help gurus urging people to get in touch with their feelings, express their passions, reconnect with their inner toddler, and in general, toss that rotten ol' Western linear masculinist rationalism overboard, uncork all their bottled-up emotions, and run barefoot and free through the Cow Pasture of Life.

Do *not* listen to these people.

There is a good reason why *Star Trek's* Mr. Spock let his emotions out only once every seven years, and an even better reason why that episode was called "Amok Time."

Getting a little wild or a bit misty is perfectly acceptable at weddings, funerals and most major holidays other than Arbor Day. But if you cannot control your emotions, they will control you, and they have a way of grabbing the steering wheel at the worst possible times and giving it a good, hard yank. Some of the most entertaining tales of boobery that cross my desk are a direct result of someone losing his cool. Here is what can happen to people who allow themselves to get flustered, frustrated, infuriated or just plain bumfuzzled...

> • A jittery man entered a convenience store in Waco, Texas, plunked down a $20 bill and asked for change. When the clerk opened the register, the man pulled a gun, grabbed all the cash in the drawer and ran. The register contained $15. The nervous thief left his $20 bill behind on the counter. He paid $20 for $15 worth of change. That's a high markup, even for a convenience store.

• In Little Rock, Arkansas, two men entered a small store, raised a rifle and demanded all the money in the register. But the clerk kept *her* cool and asked them, "Why would anyone want to go to prison over a measly $30?" The question so stumped the flustered robbers that they lowered their rifle and walked out. And probably went across the street to Neiman Marcus.

• A Port St. John, Florida, man lost his temper and vandalized his estranged wife's car. Police began chasing him. Still not thinking clearly, he climbed a barbed wire fence and took refuge in a truly unwise hiding place: on top of a power plant transformer. There was a loud boom and a puff of smoke as 50,000 volts went through him, and he came running out on fire. He became the first person in Florida to be electrocuted for petty vandalism, but probably not the last.

• A London judge warned a 49-year-old stepfather that he could "go directly to jail" for allegedly punching his 13-year-old stepson while yelling "You have ruined my life!" because the boy beat him at Monopoly. It was the culmination of a series of defeats at the hands of either the boy or his 11-year-old sister, after one of which the stepdad overturned the table and sent plates flying. His wife tried to stop it by throwing away the Monopoly game, but he just dug it back out of the trash. She described her husband as a "sore loser" at Monopoly. He's also a loser at the game of Life.

• Two burglars crept into an empty bar in Costa Blanca, Spain, but their movements activated a Big Mouth Billy Bass, one of those stupid singing rubber fish, that was mounted on the wall. Billy suddenly burst out singing "Take Me To The River." The burglars were so startled, they fled empty-handed. Too bad, since the bar owner had been hoping someone would steal that Big Mouth Billy Bass.

• Customs officers captured a dangerous fugitive who was trying to cross from the Ukraine into Slovakia. He had hired a plastic surgeon to disguise him by attaching fake ears, but the doctor used a cheap Russian-made glue instead of the high-quality American ear glue we all have in our own homes. When the crook arrived at Customs, he got nervous, started to sweat...and his ears fell off. This is another reason why Mr. Spock always had to keep his cool.

Of course, criminals live a high-stress lifestyle, so you might expect them to become nervous or flustered. But letting your emotions cloud your thinking is a pitfall that can trip up anyone, no matter how noble his intentions...

• A Massachusetts couple hosted their own cable access show to find homes for stray cats. During one broadcast, the technician let the tape roll too long, and viewers were treated to three minutes of footage of the man getting frustrated with a dozen kittens that wouldn't hold still and railing profanely at them. Upset viewers complained that he used the "F-word" about 50 times and accused him of verbal abuse of cats. He was eventually allowed back on the air after pleading that he had been having a really bad day. As would anyone who was trying to herd a dozen cats.

• Some parents in Fowey, England, hired a professional clown to perform at their six-year-old's birthday party. But the clown claimed they were the rudest kids he had seen in 17 years of clowning; they ran around, screamed, pushed and punched him, and called him a "fat pig" for 45 minutes until he just snapped and started telling them off. The parents countered that he had arrived angry about the traffic and repeatedly told the kids that they were "horrible, ignorant and ill-educated." Even more upsetting than the profanity, their kids were called "ill-educated" by someone who went to Clown College.

• A Minnesota man lost $50 at a casino in Wisconsin and was so afraid to admit it to his wife, he panicked and tried faking a mugging to cover up his gambling loss. He wasn't aware that a parking lot surveillance camera was taping him as he beat himself up. He banged his head on a light pole, smeared dirt on his face, checked himself in his truck mirror, decided he didn't look beaten enough, then banged his head on the pole some more. He ended up facing a $10,000 fine and up to nine months in jail for making a false crime report. Plus another 10-to-20 years for mugging himself.

• A woman in Johnson City, Tennessee, sued the local J.C. Penney hair salon after she went in for a haircut and the stylist trimmed her waist-length hair to just above her shoulders. The hysterical customer claimed this new hairstyle "ruined" her life, and she demanded $10.5 million to compensate her for her suffering. After six years of legal wrangling, a judge threw out the case, probably because by that time, her hair was waist-length again.

• A middle-aged woman in West Sussex, England, heard a strange sound at her home and thought burglars were drilling into a building next door. Panicked, she called the police, who rushed over but couldn't find anything. However, they could hear the noise inside her house and tracked it to her bedroom. It was coming from a vibrating sex toy that had gotten switched on inside her dresser. Police said they tried very hard to keep a straight face because they felt so sorry for the embarrassed woman. Now, when her neighbors call the police to report hearing a woman screaming, they just let it go.

• A Fulton, New York, man bought his wife a $3 pair of lime green panties at a chain clothing store, and they shrank in the wash. The store refused to refund his three bucks, so he called the police. The store owners caved in and paid him a $36 settlement, but barred him from the store. That made him even angrier, so he came back anyway, and was arrested for trespassing. Fourteen months after buying the $3 panties, he was still railing and protesting outside the store and demanding to be allowed back in. This is how pathetic you can become when you get your panties in a bunch.

As all these stories illustrate, losing your cool can leave you looking pretty silly. But there is a corollary to this rule, which is:

"Don't be too nonchalant."

Your boss may not promote you if you freak out over every little problem you are asked to deal with, but by the same token, he probably will not be any more impressed with you if you show up to the Monday morning meeting with your wife's lime green panties on your head and you don't even seem to notice.

Loser Corollary #7(A) can be summed up as *"You snooze you lose."* Two quick illustrations...

• Police in Albuquerque, New Mexico, arrested an 18-year-old male on suspicion of car theft, although he didn't even get out of the driveway. He allegedly broke into a 1983 Camaro late one night and fell asleep at the wheel before he could get it started. The owner found him the next morning, slumped over and snoozing in the passenger seat. The cops woke him up and arrested him. Either he was too lackadaisical about his job, or he was overcome by the lingering pot fumes that permeate every 1983 Camaro.

• Workers at a nail salon in Hong Kong refused to leave when a fire broke out on the roof. They were warned twice that they could be killed, but the shop owner said there was a big crush before Chinese New Year's so there was no time to reschedule those customers, and besides, acrylic nails don't look nice if you stop in the middle. So the nail artists continued working on the customers' nails for an hour while firefighters battled a blaze all around them. They didn't even charge extra for the baked-on finish.

So we see that in rare cases, it is possible to be *too* unflappable. As it says in the Bible, or in some book, anyway (this one, for instance), "What doth it profiteth a manicurist to paint every customer's nails if the customers all die of smoke inhalation before they can leaveth a tip?"

A balance must be struck, but in general, it is better to fall closer to the cool end of the emotional spectrum than to land on the hot end and run around in circles with your tuchus on fire.

As Rudyard Kipling might have said, had he been acquainted with today's cutthroat corporate culture, "If you can keep your head when all about you are losing theirs and blaming it on you, then you can get promoted over them all and fire those backstabbing weasels. And — which is more — you'll be a manager, my son!"

HALLMARK #8: CLAIM TALENTS YOU DON'T REALLY HAVE

These days, the ability to do many things at once is highly valued. "Multi-tasking," "having it all," "superwoman," "hyphenates" (i.e., "Lawyer-author," "Webmaster-interior designer," "Pet mortician-chili cook-off champion") — all these terms relate to the idea of having more than one skill, and all have become a common part of what actually passes for conversation these days.

Some rare individuals really are good at multi-tasking. Sammy Davis Jr. was often called the "World's Greatest Entertainer" because he could do practically anything well: sing, dance, act, perform sketch and standup comedy, do impressions, and just when you thought he'd run out of talents, he'd strap on a holster and do gun-twirling tricks. He even wrote *two* best-selling autobiographies. Most of us would be lucky to eke out one autobiography, but Sammy had too much material for just one life story.

Yet for all the value our society places on being multitalented, it has become increasingly difficult to find anyone who can do even one thing very well. Really good babysitters are as rare as polka-dotted zebras. People who are lucky enough to have found one honest, top-notch auto mechanic will guard his identity with a deathlike silence that would make a Buckingham Palace guard sound like a tobacco auctioneer. And don't tell me you've never stared at a ballot in a voting booth and muttered, "Over 300 million Americans, and there's nobody better qualified than this to be President?!"

Working in a showbiz-related field, I have lost count of all the fools I've had to suffer over the years who thought they had talents they clearly didn't have: the boss's son-in-law who fancied himself a screenwriting genius and kept me imprisoned in his office for an hour while he explained the term "high concept" in excruciating detail; the girlfriend-of-a-friend who imagined herself to be a singer and forced me to listen, with a horrible fixed smile on my face, to a demo tape that sounded like someone giving a walrus a high colonic; the egomaniacal video producer I worked with at a Fortune 100 corporation who insisted that she had more "visual imagination" than anyone else in the company and proved it by filling an entire training video with a cheesy and baffling "spinning dice" special effect (I never did figure out what she was training people to do, other than maybe shoot craps); and the aspiring comedy writer who thought the best way to get me to hire him was to send me a profane e-mail saying that we needed him because our jokes "suck." I wrote back congratulating him on his original and witty riposte, but suggested he attend charm school before ever again applying for any job of any kind. I also pointed out that we do not "suck." We "rule."

Sadly, the fact that it is extremely rare to find someone who can do *anything,* much less everything, does not stop people from trying to display talents and abilities they simply do not have. At its least harmful level, this merely results in amusingly bad community theater. But when the urge to pad your resume or display your multiple talents stretches beyond the safe confines of the Pepper Pot Dinner Playhouse, then you had better make sure you actually have these skills before you stand up in front of the world and demonstrate them. Otherwise, things can get ugly...

• Police in Addis Ababa, Ethiopia, arrested a faith healer who told women he could cure any disease by sucking their breasts. He actually persuaded three women to pay him for this "therapy." He did manage to cure them of ever trusting men again.

• At a party in New Jersey, a man wanted to demonstrate a cool party trick, so he loaded a rifle with cigarette butts and paper wadding and fired it at his roommate. Three of the butts penetrated the roommate's ribcage just above his heart, killing him. The would-be party entertainer was charged with manslaughter. My advice: hire a tobacco company lawyer who is willing to argue that cigarettes *can't* kill people.

• A woman in England filed indecent assault charges against a masseur who rubbed her the wrong way. She had gone to an alternative therapy center to try their massage cure for headaches, but she claimed her masseur, who was blind, massaged her breast instead of her head. Either he's a very bad masseur, or he thought she had a really soft head and a button nose.

• San Francisco passed a law banning "size discrimination," but it became a laughingstock when the first offender charged was the prestigious San Francisco Ballet School. They required applicants to have a "well-proportioned, slender body," and the parents of one little girl who was rejected filed charges against the school with the city's Human Rights Commission for not letting short, fat girls be ballerinas. Now, their recitals must look like the dancing hippo sequence in *Fantasia.*

• A man in Germany wanted to cook sausages for himself and his girlfriend, but the gas at his house had been turned off. Undeterred, he hooked up his gas cooker directly to the main gas line by himself. His girlfriend rewarded his self-proclaimed handyman skills with an offer of a cigarette. The resulting explosion injured them and five other people and destroyed the house. They weren't expecting the house to fill with deadly gas until *after* they'd eaten the sausages.

• A self-styled "miracle healer" from Hong Kong spent her life savings to go to Chile, where she declared that she would heal the hole in the ozone layer by staring at the sun seven hours a day for 49 days. Let's hope she has better luck healing the holes in her retinas.

• A Virginia woman sued a shopping mall for sexual discrimination after she was fired from her dream job of playing Santa Claus and replaced with a man. The combination of her fake beard, her breasts and her high-pitched "Ho-Ho-Ho's" confused children, who kept crying, "He's a woman!" She was offered an alternative job as an elf but quit after one day, complaining that it wasn't the same. Those elf tights were too darned effeminate.

• A cuckolded husband in Khabarovsk, Russia, wanted to kill his wife and her lover, and he decided to save a few dollars by doing the job himself. He built a homemade bomb and attached it to the door of his rival's apartment. Being unsure of his bomb-making skills, however, he decided to try a test run. He blew himself to bits, but at least he proved he did know how to build a bomb.

• A man in Bournemouth, England, filed a discrimination complaint against a driving instructor school which refused to certify him after they discovered he stuttered so badly, he couldn't say the word "Stop" before a student driver plowed into something. He lost his case, possibly because by the time he said, "I object," the judge had gone home.

• An aide to Russian President Boris Yeltsin tried his hand at humanitarian relief strategy by proposing a novel new use for old intercontinental ballistic missiles. He suggested they fill up the nose cone of a missile with seven tons of food and other relief supplies, and when an emergency occurred in an isolated part of the world, just lob the missile at it. He didn't explain how the supplies would survive the impact; but since the people he was lobbing it at wouldn't survive the impact, either, it hardly mattered.

• A 65-year-old woman in Bad Muender, Germany, attempted to embark on a new, late-life career as a bank robber. She entered a bank with tights pulled over her head and a gun in her hand, but the teller refused to believe that the granny-like thief was serious. She fired four shots into the ceiling to prove it, and he finally handed over $1,500. But she drove her getaway car so slowly, the police arrested her before she got very far. It's hard to drive a getaway car fast when you can't see over the steering wheel.

Even people who are talented enough to become top Hollywood stars can feel the need to prove they have talents beyond those that made them famous. This has led to a number of hilariously campy abominations, ranging from the song stylings of William Shatner to the novels of Ethan Hawke. But special woe be unto the celebrity who boasts of a nonexistent talent in a field unrelated to entertainment...

• In a much-ballyhooed interview with ABC's Barbara Walters, Kelly Preston declared that the golden touch enjoyed by herself and husband John Travolta was no fluke, because their deep study of Scientology had taught them to make such good career and business decisions. Just two days later, their most recent film, the Scientology-inspired megaflop *Battlefield Earth,* won seven Golden Raspberry Awards for the worst in cinema, including Razzies for Travolta as "Worst Actor" and Preston as "Worst Supporting Actress." Its seven Razzies tied an ignominious record set by *Showgirls,* whose stars and creators were more likely to attribute their career decisions to Satan than to L. Ron Hubbard.

• During the stock market boom of the 1990s, Barbra Streisand boasted that she was spending more time daytrading than singing and had become a whiz at picking stocks. Soon, friends were begging for tips, and magazines were running articles trumpeting her self-proclaimed financial acumen and dubbing her "Money Girl." This lasted until a New York tabloid analyzed her stock picks and claimed that they actually lost money during a period in which even a basic S&P Index fund would have shown a profit. No wonder she charges $350 a ticket for her concerts.

Sometimes, the dangers of multi-tasking come not from the "task" but from the "multi" side of the equation. What trips people up is not that they try to do new and difficult tasks that are beyond their capabilities, but that they try to do too many seemingly easy, everyday tasks at the same time...

• The National Highway Traffic Safety Administration held hearings in Washington to highlight the dangers of distracted drivers. For example, one man was spotted on Interstate 95, driving and talking on a cell phone, while shaving. However, women participants argued that women were better drivers because men can't resist buying every new gadget but are not as good at multi-tasking as women, who are used to checking their makeup while changing a baby while talking on the phone. While driving.

• The defenders of multi-tasking women drivers were proved wrong by a mom from Houston, Texas, who was jailed after she drove off the road, ran over a sign and crashed into a fence. She was distracted because her baby had started crying, so she lifted her shirt and tried to breast-feed the child while driving. Luckily, nobody was badly injured, but it did prove once again that drinking and driving don't mix.

• Pravda reported that a couple in Ruzayevka, Russia, had a freak accident due to poorly conceived multi-tasking. The woman was giving her boyfriend oral sex in the kitchen while he was frying pancakes. At a particularly distracting moment, he dropped the cast iron frying pan on her head. She gritted her teeth in pain, severely biting his penis. They both ended up in the hospital, the woman with a concussion and the man with stitches in his flapjack. The moral: if you want to show your gratitude to a man for helping out with the cooking, wait until he's finished.

Even corporations can fall into the trap of claiming abilities they don't really have, usually by overstating the benefits of their products...

• A New Jersey company admitted no wrongdoing but agreed to pay nearly $300,000 to settle state charges that it used false information to sell a "permanent hair replacement system." Their ads claimed it was 98.1 percent successful. This was not surprising, since it involved gluing a toupee directly to the customer's scalp. Combine that with a nail gun, and they could have claimed it was 100 percent successful.

• In an unusual consumer protection case, the owner of two adult video stores in England was ordered to pay $8,800 in damages and court costs because his videos weren't dirty enough. Customers griped that his tapes were labeled "hard core," but were really only soft core. He pleaded guilty to four offenses under the Trading Standards Act after authorities searched his shops and found no hard core porn, only soft core titles such as "Talk Naughty To Me." That was just a lot of cursing, and his customers could do that for themselves when they discovered they'd paid for a video with no hard core porn in it.

• The Digital Freedom Network gives annual awards to companies that create the worst Internet censorship software. Nominees invariably boast that their software is more effective because it censors every conceivable offensive term, which can result in embarrassing unintended consequences. Among the recent winners (or losers) was software that barred a woman from using her own name, Hillaryanne, because the word "Aryan" was in the middle of it. Another program rejected everyone named Heather because the name contains the phrase "eat her." The first prize went to some drug-screening software that barred a student from accessing his high school's website because it had the word "high" in it. Let's hope that student never has to do a research paper on "The High Court Under Bush."

Of course, as anyone who's ever suffered through hearing a Republican congressman singing "Soul Man" with a lounge band at a political fundraiser can attest, politicians and government bureaucrats are not immune to the urge to branch out and show us their many heretofore unknown talents...

• City officials in Nottingham, England, tried to show their artistic side by building a huge glass sculpture that resembled a giant magnifying glass. Engineers tried to warn them that when the sun was at the right angle, it would generate the heat of 40 electrical fires, make litter burst into flames and instantly barbecue any pigeons that flew through it. But the city leaders built it anyway. It is now the only public art in the world that regular people actually get a kick out of looking at.

While bureaucrats get scorched for exercising artistic talents they don't really have, people who are already professional artists seldom have this problem. Ironically, art is the one field in which claiming to have talent yet not having any is no drawback at all. Indeed, for some forms of the arts — such as rap music, avant-garde sculpture or "folk art" — success is almost totally dependent upon how loudly you proclaim your own brilliance. Actually *having* talent would just get in the way of your success. It might lead you to paint pictures that look like something, or to write melodic songs with sophisticated lyrics, both of which are surefire tickets to a permanent day job at Wal-Mart.

Consider these three stories, then I'll ask you a question about them all..

• Controversial artist Damien Hirst, famous for his dismembered cows floating in formaldehyde, created a new work for a London gallery out of the debris left over from the opening party: a pile of empty beer bottles, dirty ashtrays, coffee cups and food wrappers. When the janitor came in, he just sighed at the huge mess and cleaned it up. Alarmed gallery employees retrieved it from the trash bags and recreated it from photos. Hirst said he thought it was "fantastic, very funny." The janitor said, "I didn't think for a second that it was a work of art. It didn't much look like art to me."

• In the early 1990s, a woman in Glencoe, Illinois, had a front lawn full of tree stumps, kitchen cabinets and a rusty car. When the city told her to remove it, she claimed it was a work of art entitled *The Monument To Humanity No One Will Be Able To Build After George Bush Has His Winnable Nuclear War With 20 Million Americans Acceptable Loss.* An unimpressed judge decided not to wait for the nuclear bombs to clear it away and ordered her to clean up her yard.

• A man took his three kids to an art museum in Birmingham, England. They entered a room that looked like a deserted office, and his kids spied a pack of mints on the desk and ate them. It turned out the whole room was an "installation artwork" on the theme of isolation, and the way the mints had been placed just-so on the desk supposedly "dealt with social and cultural issues." The family was scolded and ejected, but the dad admitted, "It was hard not to laugh."

All right, here's the question: Are these stories about artists who don't really have the artistic talent they claim to have? Or are they stories about a janitor, a judge and three children who have an astute talent for art criticism they're not even aware of?

If you can answer that one, then you have more talent for analysis than I do. But do yourself a favor: don't go around bragging about it.

HALLMARK #9: LEAN OVER TOO FAR BACKWARD

In his 1939 book, *Fables For Our Time*, James Thurber told a fable about a bear who would drink mead, knock over the furniture and pass out drunk on the floor. Eventually, he gave up booze, became a famous temperance crusader, and demonstrated his newfound health by doing cartwheels in the living room, knocking over the furniture and passing out exhausted on the floor. The moral was, "You might as well fall flat on your face as lean over too far backward," and this advice is even more timely today. In fact, if your teenager insists on getting a tattoo, this quotation would be an excellent choice.

I have saved this Loser Hallmark for last because, while there have always been people prone to leaning over too far backward — i.e., going overboard to avoid offending anyone, overreacting to minor problems and making them worse, or in general, swatting the fly on their noses with a 20-pound sledgehammer — it was only in recent years that it became an epidemic. It threatens to undermine our social order, not to mention making common sense seem as obsolete as an 8-track tape of whaling songs. With the rise of political correctness, the oversensitive "victim culture" and the nuisance lawsuit, Americans' senses of humor and proportionality have come under assault from niggling nitwits nagging us over nothing.

Let me be clear that I am not defending blatantly offensive behavior. I'm not suggesting that you interrupt the Sunday sermon to recite the old limerick about the man from Nantucket, and even rappers have cut back on using the N-word every time they need a rhyme for "trigger." What I am talking about is the irrational, paralyzing fear still gripping some people that every problem is an urgent crisis and everyone else on the planet is either so sensitive or so stupid that he (or she, or indeterminate gender) must be handled with kid gloves and soothed with words as safe, puffy and unsubstantial as cotton candy, lest s/he/it shatter like a glass Christmas ornament.

A famous example of this was provided by the chief editor at the Reuters news service, who brought worldwide ridicule down on his head by admonishing his reporters not to refer to the hijackers who murdered thousands of innocent people at the World Trade Center as "terrorists" because we wouldn't want to offend the delicate sensibilities of people who support terrorism. After all, he clucked, "One man's 'terrorist' is another man's 'freedom fighter.'" Just as one man's "news editor" is another man's "blithering idiot."

The father (or "parent," to use the gender-neutral term — wouldn't want to offend anyone) of leaning-over-backwardism is the political correctness movement. This is the belief that in order to prove you are not prejudiced in any way, you must treat every member of every identity group (i.e., every race, religion, sex, sexual orientation, hair color, ass width, etc.) as if he, or she, or it, were a retarded two-year-old.

I'm sorry, I meant to say a "mentally-challenged two-year-old."

No, wait, I should have said a "differently-abled two-year-old!"

You can see the problem: by the time I figure out what to call him that doesn't offend anyone, he'll be a 40-year-old.

If you are going to instill this kind of neurotic dithering into an entire society, you have to start spooning it into people's skulls when they are young, which is why America's schools have become the breeding ground for so much horrendous PC flapdoodle. And there is no better example of the kind of knee-jerk, one-size-fits-all overreaction reflex rampant in schools today than the infamous "Zero Tolerance Policy."

(Take a moment to ponder the logic of school officials who are hell-bent on teaching every child "tolerance," but feel this can only be accomplished through a zero tolerance policy.)

Let's examine just one aspect of zero tolerance, the attempt to keep guns out of schools. Sounds like a reasonably laudable objective. Most of us would prefer not to be shot in the cafetorium, or any other body part, for that matter. But let's see how far afield from the goal we can get by careening overboard like an elephant on roller skates...

> • An eight-year-old boy in Green Bay, Wisconsin, was suspended from school for a day for violating the ban on replica firearms. His frighteningly realistic weapon? A key chain shaped like a toy gun. It was plastic and one-and-a-half inches long. As if that weren't scary enough, he could have put somebody's eye out with those keys.

> • The assistant principal at a middle school in Austell, Georgia, suspended an 11-year-old girl for ten days for violating the zero tolerance policy on weapons by bringing a chain to school. It was a thin, 10-inch chain attached to her Tweety Bird wallet. Tweety was not the only Loony Tune in that school.

> • A kindergarten in Nelson, New Zealand, banned children from shooting pretend guns at each other unless they first applied to the teacher for a pretend gun license. When applicants were under four, their parents were notified. Before they could be issued a pretend gun license, the children were forced to defend their need for a pretend gun. I assume if they fired a pretend gun without a pretend license, their index fingers would be confiscated.

> • School officials in Irvington, New Jersey, had two second-grade boys arrested for making terroristic threats after they folded pieces of paper and pointed them at each other like guns while playing cops and

robbers. The police chief said parents may complain that they went overboard by arresting two eight-year-olds with paper guns, but what would they say if the school ignored it and the boys got the idea to obtain a real gun? You know, like all the cool guns they saw when they were hauled down to the police station.

• An 11-year-old boy in Huntingtown, Maryland, was suspended from his middle school for saying the word "gun." He was talking to some friends about a shooting in the news, and the school bus driver overheard him and reported him. Not only was he questioned by the principal and a sheriff's deputy, but his dad claimed the police wanted to search their home without a warrant. He refused, but he had to fill out a four-page police questionnaire. All because his son simply said the word "gun." I suppose it never occurred to all these public officials that they live in a place called "HUNTING-town."

• A teenager in Keg River, Canada, was suspended from school after he confessed that he'd had a *dream* about punching his gym teacher. He should have known that when you attend public school, you are expected to give up all your dreams.

• A 7-year-old boy from Brooklyn Park, Maryland, was suspended from school for two days for allegedly nibbling a Pop Tart into what his teacher thought was the shape of a gun. The kid said he was trying to bite it into the shape of a mountain, but his teacher saw a flat, jelly-filled gun. Following this Rorschach incident, the school sent a note to parents to let them know a counselor has been hired to offer free therapy to any children who were traumatized by seeing a debatably gun-shaped toaster pastry. It sounds as if the school should offer its free therapy to the teacher and hire a nutritionist for the kids.

• School administrators in Jonesboro, Arkansas, suspended a first-grader for three days for violating the zero tolerance policy on weapons because he pointed a breaded chicken finger in the cafeteria and said, "Pow, pow, pow!" His mother argued that while school cafeteria food might be lethal, it is not a lethal weapon, and his alleged "gun" was "just a piece of chicken." But the principal replied, "It's not the object in the hand, it's the thought in the mind. Is a plastic fork worse than a metal fork? Is a pencil a weapon?" Of course, a pencil is not a weapon. Unless you sharpen it. Then he'll expel you.

Note the frighteningly offhand admission that the goal is not to remove actual weapons from kids' hands, but to censor unsanctioned thoughts from their minds, with school officials proudly assuming the role of self-appointed thought police. Well, here's a thought that principal certainly would not approve:

Perhaps a pencil is a weapon, when you use it to write antigun policies that are so stupid and repressive, they actually make kids want to shoot school officials.

I could go on and on with these anecdotes — indeed, I have so many, I considered writing a book of nothing *but* boneheaded school administrator stories, to be entitled, *Our Schools Are Run By Morons* — but unless you are as dense as an assistant vice principal, you probably got the point already. All these officials prove is Pollyanna's dictum that if you only go looking for the worst in people, you will surely find it.

But you don't have to assume that everyone around you is a homicidal maniac, just one chicken finger or Pop Tart away from a shooting spree, to go overboard and become a first class noodge and an A-1 laughingstock. You can also achieve that goal by overindulging your low opinion of other people's intelligence and assuming that everyone except you is so mentally-deficient that without your constant protection, they might poke their eyes out with a fork while trying to eat soup.

Nowhere is this more evident than in the ever-expanding warning labels and instruction sheets found on even the simplest of products. I first noticed this trend over 20 years ago, when I read the cooking directions on a microwave lasagna box which said to microwave the entree on "High" for 10 minutes, then remove it from the oven. The maker felt compelled to add, "Use oven mitts!"

I thought at the time that the warning was absurd, since anyone who didn't already know to use oven mitts when handling something that had just been nuked in a microwave for 10 minutes would be far too brain-damaged to be able to read. I assumed this was an aberration; however, with my constant perusal of the news, it became apparent that it was merely the first noodle in a giant lasagna of condescension...

• The Carmarthenshire County Council in England wanted to prevent any confusion about their new road safety rules, so their official rule booklets included definitions of various words which the poor, stupid public might not understand. Among them were "children," "pedestrian" and "daylight," helpfully defined as "all times other than darkness." As opposed to "living daylights," defined as "what will be beaten out of you if you keep talking down to people."

• The Doncaster, England, Town Council ordered maintenance workers to attend seminars on how to climb a ladder and how to change a light bulb. One school janitor complained that he felt as if he were in a comedy film — sitting in a class, watching a teacher demonstrate how to screw in different-sized light bulbs, and feeling "like a complete idiot." All he learned was that the best way to get rid of dim bulbs is to elect a new Town Council.

• Warning labels have become so ridiculous, a group called Michigan Lawsuit Abuse now gives out annual "Wacky Warning Label" awards. Some of their finalists include a toilet with a label warning consumers not to drink the water in it (although they didn't say you couldn't use it for bathing). There was also an electric wood router whose label read, *"WARNING! This product not intended for use as a dental drill"* (unless you're George Washington's dentist). The winner was the maker of some bicycle shin pads whose package warned, *"Shin pads cannot protect any part of the body they do not cover!"* I guess if you want the magical "Shin Pads of Invulnerability," you have to pay extra.

To be fair, manufacturers are under enormous pressure to warn against every possible danger, no matter how unlikely *("Warning: Do not use toaster while showering!")* for fear that if they don't, some chucklehead will actually do it, then sue the maker for not explicitly warning the public that water and electrical appliances are not a healthy combo.

The problem is that if you warn of the dangers of absolutely everything, you defeat the purpose. If everything is equally dangerous, then nothing is particularly dangerous. America now has the world's longest warning labels, some rolling on for page after page of tiny print, the result being that nobody bothers to read them anymore. It's too hard to sort out which warnings are really there to protect the consumer and which ones are there only to protect the manufacturer from lawsuits. It doesn't matter how inclusive the warning is; if nobody reads it, it is the same as if there were no warning label at all. In short, they bent over so far backward, they came full circle and met themselves coming the other way, a feat of contortion you usually only see at Cirque de Soleil.

Another shining example of counter-productive over-protectiveness comes to us courtesy of the federal government, not surprising considering that we keep electing lawyers to write our laws, which is like hiring kleptomaniacs to run our banks (actually, I think we did that, too.)

Whenever a car commercial airs on the radio, it always ends with a rapid-fire legal disclaimer of approximately 25,000 words squeezed into ten seconds. This is because the government, in bending over backward to protect the hapless, waif-like car buyer, has mandated that all automobile ads must contain specific information about tax, title, license fees and a dozen other details which could easily be found in the buyer's contract, if the poor sap would bother to read it before signing it. The same laws force advertisers to mention every possible side effect of a drug. This mandate might work for print ads, or even TV ads, where the advertiser gets around it by printing the disclaimer in a type font so small, it could hide behind an amoeba.

But on radio, this voluminous disclaimer must be read out loud by an announcer. Reading it at an understandable pace would take at least two minutes, and not even the best intentions of federal bureaucrats can compress space and time to fit two minutes into a 30-second commercial. So the producers electronically speed it up until it is a dense, 10-second block of absolutely indecipherable super-gibberish, the words blasting into your face like leaves from a leaf blower. Instead of helping the consumer, this forces the advertiser to leave out information that might actually be useful to consumers, just to make time for a wad of baffling babble that nobody can understand — except perhaps politicians, who are the only people on earth who can babble gibberish faster than an announcer on a car commercial.

Our final species of limbo artist, and one that has become far too prevalent in recent years, is the social justice warrior. These persons believe themselves to be so politically or morally enlightened that it is their duty to find ways to uplift all the lesser mortals around them, and their obsession with remaking the world into their own vision of Utopia often lands them in the news and causes them to become the butt of derisive jokes. This usually occurs after they find some urgent crisis that nobody else ever considered to be a problem and blow it up to Hindenburg-like proportions...

- The animal rights group People for the Ethical Treatment of Animals seems to relish making news by ginning up faux outrage. They once called on the Green Bay Packers football team to change their name because it promoted meat packers. Showing that they are indeed true Cheeseheads, PETA suggested that the team be renamed the "Pickers," referring to picking vegetables, or possibly the "Six-Packers," in honor of Wisconsin's brewing industry. The team president said he had no interest in renaming the Packers. That was a polite way of saying that PETA could take their beef and can it.

- PETA also once called for legislation to prevent the makers of products for science students from selling a kit called "RoboRoach." It allowed budding Einsteins to surgically implant electrodes in cockroaches and control their movements. PETA argued that it was cruel and inhumane to cockroaches. We need a science kit that rewires cockroaches to talk, so they can tell PETA that if they really want to do cockroaches a favor, they should lobby for legislation to ban shoes.

- PETA did score a victory for robotic animals after they pressured Disneyland into changing its hokey "Jungle Cruise" ride after more than 40 years. The wisecracking guides were barred from firing their cap pistols to "scare away" the animatronic hippos after PETA branded it "a form of animal cruelty" (or cruelty to something in the form of animals, at least). For their next project, I suggest they lobby to get the moonshine-addicted robot bears from the "Country Bear Jamboree" into a good 12-step program.

• The Scottish Fire Service Fairness and Diversity
Forum - a group of civil servants and union leaders
dedicated to the urgent mission of eradicating sexism
in Scotland's fire departments - came out with some
practical ideas for helping female fire station
employees. For instance, they suggested scrapping
even the gender-neutral term "firefighter" because
"fighting" fires sounds too aggressive, and therefore
masculine. They also suggested scrapping the job title
of "firemaster" because it was derogatory to women.
Somehow, they forgot to suggest scrapping those
phallic fire poles that might make female "fire-
discouragers" feel like strippers.

• Officials at the University of Iowa got an e-mail
from *one* parent, complaining that the longtime
Hawkeye marching band song, "In Heaven, There Is
No Beer (That's Why We Drink It Here)," might
encourage students to become alcoholics. Band
members argued that college students hardly needed an
old polka tune to give them the idea to drink beer, but
the officials chose to ignore the majority's common
sense and bent over backward to accommodate the
lone complainant. They let the band play the song, but
barred them from singing the lyrics. Or they could
have just changed the lyrics to "In Heaven, there are no
meddlesome do-gooders and noodle-spined university
officials."

There is no doubt that in all these cases, the people who came off
looking so ridiculous were passionate, energetic and well-
intentioned. But so was Jenny McCarthy when she launched her war
on whooping cough vaccine. All they really accomplished was to
prove that the road to Hell is paved with good intentions, and
pursuing those intentions with too much passion and energy only gets
you to Hell comfortably ahead of schedule.

Like the people in Chapter 2, many lost sight of their goal, not by forgetting what the goal was, but by attacking it with such strident fervor and tunnel vision that they alienated the very people whose support they needed to achieve it. In short, they went overboard and sank themselves.

And others who sought to build a more tolerant society bent over so far backward to display their tolerance that they only managed to patronize the groups they intended to protect and generate resentment, derision, a loss of respect - you know, *"intolerance"* - in everyone else.

I can think of no better way to close this chapter than with its very own stern warning label:

"WARNING! Leaning over backward too far, too long and too often can result in the complete loss of your spine!"

POP QUIZ

Having slogged this far through the book, you have been exposed to a staggering array of chuzzlewits, lamebrains and nimrods, and you have had their simple, basic mistakes identified, analyzed and cataloged for you. It is now time to find out whether this close exposure to so much incompetence has eroded your own intelligence, or whether I have attained my goal of helping you to sharpen your thinking skills and avoid abject humiliation by learning from the mistakes of others.

That's right: it's pop quiz time!

Pick up a pencil (you don't have to write anything, but it will give you something to chew on while you're thinking) and read the following questions. The premise of each question is taken directly from a bona fide news item. You will be given a choice of two answers. Try to pick the one that sounds most sensible, logical and correct.

Ready?…Set?…*Begin!*

1. You are a fugitive living covertly in West Haven, Connecticut, and since you are wanted on charges of fraudulently taking unemployment benefits, you have no choice but to go to work. What should you do?

> A. Seek a job that doesn't require a background check or contact with cops..
>
> B. March into the police station and apply to be a cop.

2. You are a contractor who lands a job to install wrought-iron fencing around four school campuses in Scottsdale, Arizona. Alas,

you miscalculate and run out of fencing after three schools. What should you do for the fourth school?

A. Buy more wrought-iron fencing out of your own pocket and make a note to plan more carefully next time.

B. Infuriate city officials by surrounding the school with a barbed-wire fence instead.

3. You are an airline pilot who just landed in Milan, Italy. During the flight, a passenger illegally smoked in the bathroom, but nobody will admit to it. What should you do?

A. Report the incident and fly off to your next destination.

B. Fly off the handle and keep all 148 passengers hostage in the plane on the tarmac for 40 minutes, trying to sweat a confession out of somebody.

4. You are the maker of an energy bar named the best-tasting health snack by a major fitness magazine, yet you are paying to settle a $2.76 million class-action lawsuit. Why?

A. Our overly-litigious society makes settling frivolous suits more cost-efficient than fighting in court.

B. You don't have much of a defense, since someone discovered the reason your health bar tastes so good is that it has ten times as much salt and four times as much fat as you advertised.

5. You work for the US Bureau of Land Management and you need to issue some regulations on digging for geothermal power. To make sure everyone understands you, what word or words do you use to express the concept of "digging"?

A. "Digging."

B. "Commencing surface-disturbing activities."

6. You are an overly-confident confidence man who sold rare Beanie Babies for up to $1,000 on auction websites, collected the money through a mail drop under a phony name, and never delivered the merchandise. When people complain on an Internet bulletin board, what do you do?

A. Remain silent and stay out of sight.

B. Post this message for the police to trace back to you: "Ha, ha, ha, ha, ha. Never see the person, never meet the person, never speak with the person and then get upset when you get ripped off. You must be a bunch of morons."

7. You are a Mexican government official asked to attend a conference on reforming election laws. How do you and your colleagues approach this grave responsibility?

A. Seriously and soberly.

B. By ordering enough whisky, cognac, tequila, vodka and beer to run up a taxpayer-paid bar tab of $12,000, or 3,567 times the minimum daily wage for Mexican citizens (before taxes).

8. You and two friends steal a gas bottle from a store in Chumphon, Thailand, and demand that the shopkeeper pay you money to get it back. But you fail to plan for the possibility that she has no money so early in the day. What do you do?

A. Make a clean getaway and sell the gas bottle elsewhere.

B. Tell the shopkeeper that you'll wait until she's earned enough money to pay your extortion demand, then go into the back room with your gang and all go to sleep in some hammocks.

9. You would like to rob a Boston coffee shop by grabbing the cash register and running, but your leg is broken and in a full cast. Should you...

A. Wait until it heals and you can run again?

B. Grab the register, try to run on your cast, get tackled by two customers, and end up with two broken legs?

10. You are a lounge singer from Allentown, Pennsylvania and you are busted for drunk driving. What do you do?

A. Hire a really good lawyer and get acquitted.

B. Act as your own lawyer, wear a canary yellow jacket, put on a floor show for the jury, take a bow after your opening statement, argue that your slurred diction was really due to tired singing muscles, and get convicted.

11. You manufacture a common household product, and you feel it is necessary for this product to carry the stern warning label, "For exterior use only!" What product do you make?

A. An exterior house paint with dangerous fumes.

B. A lawn sprinkler.

12. You live in Manitoba, Canada, and you buy a bulletproof vest. To be certain it will really offer protection, what should you do?

A. Research the tests conducted by independent laboratories.

B. Decide that you are qualified to be a testing engineer, put on the vest, have your friends shoot you with a .22-caliber rifle and a 12-gauge shotgun, and miraculously end up in the hospital with only cracked ribs and bruises, thinking, "Hey, it works!"

13. You are the head of a successful baby food company (let's call it, say, "Glerber"), and you want to sell even more product. What should you do?

A. Use proven marketing techniques to get more parents to buy your products.

B. Introduce a line of goopy entrees for teens and package them in jars that look exactly like baby food jars, so that any teenager would be horribly embarrassed to be seen within 10 feet of them.

14. The Hall of Justice in Redwood City, California, declares zero tolerance for anything resembling a weapon, and you are the very first person busted when you enter carrying a suspicious electronic device that contains wires and a timer. What is this dangerous device?

A. A time bomb.

B. A bread maker.

15. You wish to help the Myrtle Beach, Florida, fire department with a dignified fundraising event that will *not* draw bad attention and force them to reject your donation. What do you organize?

A. A church bake sale.

B. A "Ham-Rubbing Party," in which men pay to rub a greasy ham on a topless dancer's breasts.

16. You decide to rob a motel office in Van Buren, Arkansas. How should you go about this?

A. Enter in disguise, demand the cash, and escape quickly before anyone can identify you.

B. Get nervous, dawdle around, finally rob the clerk and flee after you have already filled out a guest registration card for him with your real name and home address on it.

17. You work for Great Britain's Royal Society of Arts, Manufacture and Commerce, and you are writing guidelines for business students for a course in calling on clients. How do you express the idea that they should tell the clients how long their visits will last?

A. "Tell the clients how long your visit will last."

B. Insure that "tensions between resource constraints influencing ending and client requirements are managed."

18. You are a fugitive real estate mogul wanted for a grisly murder in Galveston, Texas. To avoid attracting attention while hiding out in Bethlehem, Pennsylvania, how do you change your looks to blend in?

A. Cut your hair and grow a full beard.

B. Wear a ridiculous-looking brown wig with a clashing white fake mustache, causing local people to crack up laughing and point at you.

19. You are in charge of planning tactical exercises for the Clarksville, Tennessee, police force. To insure that nobody is hurt, should you...

A. Find a safe, controlled environment and use only dummy weaponry?

B. Do it inside police headquarters, where someone can mistakenly lob a live tear gas bomb into a storage room, soaking all the Christmas toys collected for underprivileged children with tear gas?

20. You are a Colombian government bureaucrat charged with the goal of preventing cheaters from getting pensions in the names of dead people. Do you...

A. Set up an efficient system to cross-reference pension recipients' names with the names on official death certificates?

B. Make thousands of elderly people wait in long lines at sweltering government offices to prove they are still alive, until one of them keels over dead of old age in your waiting room while waiting for a "survival certificate"?

21. You are a blind man in Mainz, Germany, and you have had a bit too much to drink. But you have always wanted to drive a car. What should you do?

A. Accept that driving is probably not a talent you should explore, particularly when drunk.

B. Borrow a car from a friend (who must be blind drunk himself) and drive it, but stop and get out every few feet to feel around in front of the car to make sure there's nothing there you might hit.

22. You are a buxom Englishwoman, obviously well aware that you have very large breasts, and you have locked yourself out of your house. Do you...

A. Call a locksmith, knowing that he'll hurry right over, due to your very large breasts?

B. Try to wiggle through the doggie door and, due to your very large breasts, get so hopelessly stuck that the fire brigade rushes over (also due to your very large breasts) and cuts you out?

23. You are a happy groom in Hindustan, India, and you wish to celebrate your wedding with an adult beverage. When should you start drinking?

A. At the reception, sharing champagne with your lovely bride.

B. Just before the ceremony, so you can show up stinking drunk, insult all the guests and get hauled away by the police, leaving your bride to marry a sober wedding guest who steps up and proposes in your place.

24. As a trainer of seeing-eye dogs in Germany, you have a dog named Lucky who killed his first owner by leading him in front of a bus, killed the second by leading him off a pier, nudged the third off a railroad platform in front of a speeding train, and killed his fourth by abandoning him in heavy traffic. What do you do with Lucky?

A. Rename him "Unlucky" and palm him off on some sharp-eyed sucker whom he can't kill.

B. Decide that it's more important not to waste the time spent training him than it is to help blind people stay alive and start hunting for a fifth blind owner.

25. You enter a seafood restaurant in Washington State with your jaws wired shut and order clam chowder put through a blender so you can drink it with a straw. The waiter replies that he can't do this because their kitchen doesn't have a blender. What do you do next?

A. Order a cup of broth or a milkshake instead.

B. Throw a raging temper tantrum, hurl your bicycle through the restaurant's front window and get charged with a felony, thus demonstrating that it's not surprising someone broke your jaw.

26. You and your comrades are all soldiers in the Colombian army, facing a harsh war against tough leftist guerrillas. The army gives you money for food. What do you spend it on?

A. Food.

B. Alcohol and prostitutes, which leaves you so hungry, drunk, hung over and sexually exhausted that the guerrillas deal your army its worst defeat in 30 years.

27. You are an Akron, Ohio, husband who has decided to electrocute his wife. How would you go about this?

A. Get a hair dryer with a long cord and toss it into her bath water.

B. Get a hair dryer, don't bother checking the length of the cord, try to toss it into her bath water, discover that the cord is too short to reach, and get arrested after your wife calls the police while you are still searching for an extension cord.

28. You are driving down the highway near Boca Raton, Florida, when you hit a pedestrian who flies through the air, crashes through your windshield, and lands in the seat beside you, lying motionless and injured. What should you do?

A. Rush him to the nearest hospital.

B. Lose your temper, demand that he get out of your car, and when he doesn't respond, pummel him for two miles until you finally shove him out the door.

29. You are a member of any one of several university research teams, and your latest discoveries include one of the following: Teenage boys who are sexually active are less likely to be depressed than boys who are virgins; most Americans would rather win the lottery than catch herpes; elderly drivers make slower left turns than younger drivers; people who get lots of sex are generally happier than people on Death Row; and ice cream is far more popular than broccoli. What do you do with this information?

A. Bury it and try to think of a new survey topic that won't subject you to global ridicule.

B. Send out a press release.

30. You are a fugitive wanted in Kansas on two counts of molesting young girls. What should you do?

A. Change your name, move someplace where nobody will recognize you, and lay low.

B. Become a contestant on *Wheel of Fortune.*

ANSWER KEY

All the "A" answers are the sensible, reasonable responses a thinking person should have given. All the "B" answers are the wrong responses. They were also what the people who were involved in the original events actually did.

If you answered "B" to any of these questions, go back and read this book again.

If you were too dim to figure out that all the "B" choices were wrong before I told you, then go buy ten more copies of this book and read each one of them. Perhaps that will help.

IN CONCLUSION...

We hope this book has shown you that every human being — from third grade dropouts to captains of industry and world leaders — is prone to making the same simple, stupid mistakes over and over again. The only difference is in scale. When a dumb crook does it, it's amusing. When banks and CEOs do it, it's recessionary. When the government does it, it's Obamacare. But perhaps if you study the dumb mistakes others have made, you can learn to recognize those traps before you stick your own foot into them, and thereby avoid having to gnaw your leg off to get out.

If you've learned nothing from this book, then at least you've enjoyed the warm glow that comes from realizing people far more wealthy and powerful than you will ever be have, at one time or another, bollixed themselves up far worse than you ever did. For example, once, during a real estate recession in New York, Donald Trump was rumored to be $1 billion in debt. How could that *not* make you feel good? I'll bet your debts aren't *half* that.

And if you've *really* learned nothing from this book, and you go out and repeat all Nine Hallmarks of the Highly Incompetent Loser yourself, then at least you've greatly increased your chances of hearing your name mentioned on the radio. Should that happen, please accept my heartfelt thanks in advance for keeping us in business.

ABOUT THE AUTHORS...

Pat Reeder has worked in virtually every communications medium. He has written training videos and other materials for such top corporations as GTE, Sylvania, Video Logic, Southwestern Bell and DLM Inc. He has been a major market radio DJ and production director, writer/voice on countless comedy radio commercials, and head writer of the syndicated radio service, *The Morning Punch.* He also worked with Gov. Mike Huckabee to write *The Huckabee Report,* the most successful short daily national feature in radio, heard three times daily on over 500 stations nationwide. As original head writer for the Lyons Group, he co-wrote the first episodes of *Barney the Dinosaur,* although God knows he doesn't like to talk about it. He has written stand-up material for nationally-known comedians and columns on goofy paranormal news for the *NTS Skeptic* and *Skeptical Briefs* magazines. His first book, *Hollywood Hi-Fi* (with George Gimarc) received worldwide raves and will soon be available in a new e-book update (see http://www.hollywoodhifi.net). Pat presents hilarious live presentations based on his two books.

Laura Ainsworth is not only a writer, but also a talented singer, actress, painter and cartoonist. She grew up watching her late dad, big band sax and clarinet master Billy Ainsworth, back such icons as Ella Fitzgerald and Tony Bennett. She keeps his legacy alive through her recordings and live shows. Her albums *Keep It To Yourself* and *Necessary Evil* (Eclectus Records) have received rave reviews and worldwide airplay. Her next album, *New Vintage,* is in production. Her music is available at CDBaby.com, iTunes, Amazon and other top music sites. You can also find videos, photos, free MP3s and more at www.lauraainsworth.com.

As part of her "day job," Laura has created hundreds of parody songs, as well as jingle lyrics, PR releases, ads and other materials for radio, major corporations and the US military. One interactive video sales training program won her the coveted ITVA

Golden Reel Award. An expert consultant on historic home décor and design, she has written many articles for home style magazines and also writes the popular "Welcome To The Birdhouse" column for *Companion Parrot Quarterly* magazine.

Together, Pat and Laura created and wrote *The Comedy Wire* (www.comedy-wire.com), which for years provided topical humor daily to top radio shows around the world. They now create similar material for select national radio shows and Internet podcasts, and they have been consulting writers/researchers on numerous projects, including a stage musical and two *New York Times* bestselling books. Pat and Laura purchased the Fabulous '50s house in Texas that was Laura's childhood home and restored it to its midcentury modern ginchiness. They share it with a flock of happy, squawking parrots, many of them "handicapable" or rescue birds, that keep inexplicably showing up on their doorstep.

.

www.ingramcontent.com/pod-product-compliance
Lightning Source LLC
Chambersburg PA
CBHW060943040426
42445CB00011B/987